·SKYE·

COLIN BAXTER

RICHARD DREW PUBLISHING
GLASGOW

WIDE CONTRASTS IN THE SCENERY OF SCOTLAND ALWAYS IMPRESS THE VISITOR. WHERE ELSE CAN BE FOUND IN SO SMALL AN AREA MOUNTAINS, SAVAGE SEAS, ROUGH COASTS, WOODED VALLEYS, WILD MOORLAND, TUMBLING RIVERS AND FERTILE PLAINS? CHANGING PLAY OF LIGHT BROUGHT BY THE FICKLE CLIMATE ADDS MYSTERY TO THE SCOTTISH EXPERIENCE.

NO-ONE IN RECENT YEARS HAS CAPTURED THIS EVER-CHANGING VARIETY AS SENSITIVELY AS THE PHOTOGRAPHER, COLIN BAXTER, WHO HAS IN THIS SERIES SELECTED CERTAIN AREAS AND THEMES TO CONVEY THE RICH DIVERSITY OF SCOTLAND'S CITIES AND COUNTRYSIDE.

SKYE IS MUCH MORE THAN THE LEGENDARY ISLAND OF MIST AND ROMANCE. THE MOST ACCESSIBLE OF THE WESTERN ISLES, IT ATTRACTS VISITORS IN THEIR THOUSANDS TO ITS VARIED SCENERY. THE CUILLIN, THE MOST SPECTACULAR RANGE OF MOUNTAINS IN BRITAIN, ARE AN AWESOME SIGHT TO THE PHOTOGRAPHER AND A CHALLENGE TO THE CLIMBER. THE ISLAND HAS LONG HISTORICAL ASSOCIATIONS, ESPECIALLY WITH THE MACDONALD AND MACLEOD CLANS, AND TODAY IT LOOKS TO A NEW FUTURE WHICH INCLUDES ENCOURAGE-MENT OF ITS ANCIENT GAELIC CULTURE.

FISKAVAIG BAY WITH
THE CUILLIN HILLS IN THE DISTANCE

PEAT CUTTINGS
NEAR STAFFIN

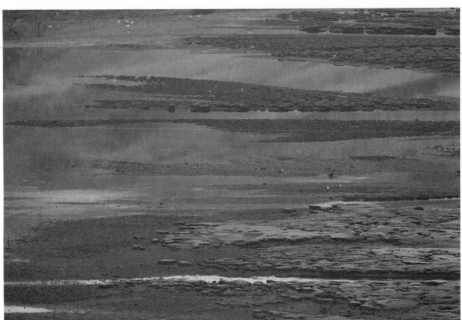

LOW TIDE AT
THE FOOT OF
LOCH HARPORT

ISLE OF SKYE
FROM ARDB/
WESTER ROS

LOCH HARPORT
AND FERNILEA

THE CUILLIN HILLS
FROM ELGOL

ISLE OF SKYE
FROM CREAG GHORM, WESTER ROSS

HAMARAMORE
WITH CUILLIN HILLS
IN THE DISTANCE

Post Offices

LOCH VATTEN AND
LOCH NA FAOLINN

SUNSET
FROM WATERNISH

"Thrift"
or "Sea Pink"

ow tide
t the foot of
och Ainort

SUNSET BEHIND
THE ISLE OF WIAY,
LOCH BRACADALE

SGURR NAN GILLEAN
AND BRUACH NA FRITHE
OPPOSITE
HEALABHAL MHOR

INNER SOUND, GLAMAIG
AND MARSCO

WATERFALL
FROM LOCH MEALT
TO THE SEA

WATERSTEIN HEA

ISAY, CLETT
AND MINGAY

PORTNALONG

TARNER ISLAND AND
HEALABHAL MHOR

LOCH HARPORT AND
THE CUILLIN HILLS

ORONSAY AND
ARDTRECK POINT

LOCH HARPORT
(NEAR PORTNALONG)

ARDTRECK POINT

"THE NEEDLE",
QUIRAING

MEALL NA SUIRAMACH,
QUIRAING

LOCH DUNVEGAN

Ard Beag,
Waternish

CROFT

ARDMORE POINT
AND
DUNVEGAN HEAD

First Published 1987 by
RICHARD DREW PUBLISHING
6 CLAIRMONT GARDENS, GLASGOW G3 7LW, SCOTLAND

Copyright © 1987 Colin Baxter

Printed and bound in Great Britain by
Blantyre Printing and Binding Co. Ltd.

British Library Cataloguing in Publication Data.

"Skye. – (Experience Scotland).
1. Skye – Description and travel –
Guide-books
1. Title   II. Series
914. 11'82 DA880.S6

ISBN 0-86267-187-6

OSCEs for

MEDICAL AND SURGICAL FINALS

Shabana A. Bora MBBS
Senior House Officer, Obstetrics and Gynaecology, Queen Mary's Hospital,
Sidcup, UK

Theresa G.H. Heah MBBS
Senior House Officer, Neurosurgery, St. George's Hospital, London, UK

Shivangi Thakore MA(Cantab) MBBS
Senior House Officer, General Practice Vocational Training, University College
London Hospitals, London, UK

Editorial Advisor:
Deborah Gill MBBS MRCGP MMEd ILTM
Senior Lecturer in Medical Education, Academic Centre for Medical Education,
University College London, London, UK

Hodder Arnold

A MEMBER OF THE HODDER HEADLINE GROUP

First published in Great Britain in 2005 by
Hodder Education, a member of the Hodder Headline Group,
338 Euston Road, London NW1 3BH

http://www.hoddereducation.co.uk

Distributed in the United States of America by
Oxford University Press Inc.,
198 Madison Avenue, New York, NY 10016
Oxford is a registered trademark of Oxford University Press

Whilst the advice and information in this book are believed to be true and accurate at
the date of going to press, neither the author[s] nor the publisher can accept any legal
responsibility or liability for any errors or omissions that may be made. In particular, (but
without limiting the generality of the preceding disclaimer) every effort has been made to
check drug dosages; however it is still possible that errors have been missed. Furthermore,
dosage schedules are constantly being revised and new side-effects recognized. For these
reasons the reader is strongly urged to consult the drug companies' printed instructions before
administering any of the drugs recommended in this book.

British Library Cataloguing in Publication Data
A catalogue record for this book is available from the British Library

Library of Congress Cataloging-in-Publication Data
A catalog record for this book is available from the Library of Congress

ISBN-10: 0 340 81589 2
ISBN-13: 978 0 340 81589 2

1 2 3 4 5 6 7 8 9 10

Commissioning Editor: Georgina Bentliff
Project Editor: Heather Smith
Production Controller: Jane Lawrence
Cover Design: Amina Dudhia
Illustrations: Beehive Illustration
Index: Dr Laurence Errington

Typeset in 9.5/12 Rotis Serif by Charon Tec Pvt. Ltd, Chennai, India
Printed and bound in Malta

What do you think about this book? Or any other Hodder Arnold title?
Please visit our website at www.hoddereducation.co.uk

CONTENTS

PREFACE

The objective structured clinical examination (OSCE) is increasingly replacing the traditional long-case, short-case and viva-based clinical finals. Although OSCE style finals are fairer than the traditional style of clinical finals, they are not a perfect assessment of competence. Diligent students, who have acquired the necessary knowledge and skills to qualify as doctors, do occasionally fail OSCE based finals. As for all examinations, exam technique has a great deal to do with success, and OSCEs have a large element of performance to them – a fact that, unfortunately, we learned through personal experience. As well as working hard, it is, therefore, also necessary to work *smart* for the final OSCE, and put on the performance the examiners are looking for.

Many clinical teachers have sat more traditional finals and may have little experience of OSCEs. There is still also an absence on the bookshelves of a user-friendly final OSCE revision guide of the form that exists for other types of clinical exams. This book is therefore a compact revision aid for final OSCEs, providing students with tips about *how to play the OSCE game and win*. It represents our combined knowledge in a format that we would have benefited from whilst preparing for our own finals. We hope it proves to be a useful revision aid, and that it allows more deserving medical students to celebrate qualifying as doctors on results day.

Remember, don't just work hard – work smart!

S. Bora
T. Heah
S. Thakore

ACKNOWLEDGEMENTS

We would like to thank Georgina Bentliff and Heather Smith of Hodder Arnold for their continued support, which made this project possible. Inexpressible thanks go to Dr Deborah Gill for her editorial advice, enthusiasm, up-to-date knowledge of medical education, and original contribution in the introductory and personal and professional development sections. Finally, we would like to thank Dr Neil Goulbourne for his factual and literary advice, and our many friends who, enthused by the idea of knowing an author and sharing our sentiment, reminded us to keep writing in between all those on-calls.

INTRODUCTORY SECTION

HOW TO USE THIS BOOK

OSCEs for Medical and Surgical Finals is aimed at the level of clinical finals and the clinical Professional and Linguistics Assessment Board (PLAB) exam. It therefore focuses on medicine and surgery, broadly excluding the other specialties, except where they may be a significant part of a medical or surgical condition, and omitting very basic clinical skills, neither of which is usually examined at this stage. It is a revision aid to be used during preparation for the final objective structured clinical examination (OSCE), and is not intended to be a complete textbook of clinical skills. We have pitched the content at a level which assumes that students using the book will already be familiar with clinical skills, and will be using it to practise in an exam-focused way for the final OSCE, gaining insight into what OSCEs are all about, what is required in each station, what the examiner will be looking for, and vital tips about how to score well. By the final year, most students do have a good repertoire of clinical skills that just need some brushing up, although it doesn't always feel like that!

The final year of medical school can leave you confused about how to structure your work. Aside from preparing for the OSCE, there is also the not so small task of revising for written finals, and at times these two demands seem conflicting. It must be stressed, however, that success in an OSCE is difficult without a fairly sound knowledge of medicine and surgery. Being able to piece together clinical signs and interpret histories obviously relies on knowing common presentations and pathologies. Although everyone is different, it is probably best to start revising for your written finals early on in the final academic year, aiming to have completed much of it before the start of the last term. At the same time you should start practising (or learning!) the clinical skills that might be tested in your OSCE; you will then be left with ample time to do the exam-focused OSCE preparation that this book facilitates. Essentially, your examiners are looking for a fluent performance – they want to see that the competencies being assessed are second nature to you. This might seem like an act that is impossible to convey, but it is not. If you go through the stations in this book over and over again until you can perform each one near perfectly, you will walk into the OSCE feeling like you can breeze through it and, if you believe that, breeze through it you will!

Revising for clinical finals is best done in pairs or threes, taking it in turns to be candidate, examiner and, if necessary, role-player. This set-up replicates the scene of the final OSCE as much as possible. It also enables someone to assess how you carry out each task and give you feedback on what you have done well and how you could improve. A valuable lesson we gained whilst revising for our OSCE was that each of us had different strengths and weaknesses in our clinical knowledge and skills, and that there was a huge amount we learnt just by observing each other perform various stations. In this regard, revising with several different people is a good idea. This group work can take place in a variety of settings: on the ward using real patients, in the clinical skills centre and at home. *OSCEs for Medical and Surgical Finals* is written to be an aid in this group revision situation, providing the 'examiner' with checklists against which to mark the 'candidate'.

The rest of this introductory section contains crucial information about the OSCE in finals – knowledge that will help you understand what a finals OSCE consists of, what form it might take, how it is marked, what sorts of cases you can be given, what competencies are being assessed, and how not to fail. Following on from this introductory section are sections on practical skills, examination, emergency situations-focused history and management, discharge planning, chronic disease management, conducting an interview with patients with mental health and cognitive problems, communication, and personal and professional development. Each section contains a section-specific introduction, giving generic advice applicable to all the stations in that section. Individual stations start with a scenario that provides candidates with the sort of instructions they would be given in an OSCE. In stations for which a role-player is required, this scenario will help inform him or her of the role to be played, as will details in the 'key tips' section for that station. Each individual station also consists of a checklist, which can be used whilst you are thinking about how to perform each task and by your 'examiner' as a mark-sheet when you are preparing in groups. At the end of each checklist are some key tips for success in that station, which will help improve your performance the next time you practise.

We were very keen for it to be a compact book, allowing you to carry it around hospital and use it opportunistically. If, for example, you should stumble across a patient with a good murmur or have a few moments to spare in your clinical skills centre, why not whip it out and pretend you're in your OSCE? Of course, you cannot always be in a group, so when you are alone you can use this book to work out in your own mind how to perform each type of skill and what individual stations require.

Most of the stations in the book are written to be approximately 7 minutes long, so if OSCE stations in your finals are longer or shorter than this, you will need to think about what will be additionally required or what should be omitted. It is most useful to practise to the time frame set out in your own medical school OSCE. Some medical schools include a global score to be given by the examiner and, if applicable, the role-player/ patient at the end of each station. In some assessments this can amount to a significant proportion of the total marks, so it is worth paying attention to it. In each chapter introduction, we describe how to score these global marks. Finally, the entirety of this book cannot be wholly applicable to every medical school, and we would encourage you to adapt these checklists where you feel appropriate and, indeed, to use them as a guide to writing others. The process of writing checklists will give you an insight into what examiners are looking for, an insight which will help you play the OSCE game and win.

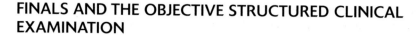

FINALS AND THE OBJECTIVE STRUCTURED CLINICAL EXAMINATION

The OSCE in finals – why?

Summative assessment is a time-consuming, difficult and expensive process to do well. It is a high-stakes occupation for all participants. The increased scrutiny of the medical profession over recent years has meant that medical schools have to be absolutely sure that graduates have real and measurable competency in the skills they will need as junior doctors. As a result, assessments have become increasingly focused on testing competencies; they now go beyond simply examining theoretical knowledge about skills – candidates must actually demonstrate the skills being assessed. It is difficult to test a medical student's performance '*in vivo*' or in real settings, as they are not yet practising clinicians. The alternative is to focus on '*in vitro*' tests such as OSCEs.

Old-style finals, although long established, had a number of weaknesses. There was an element of 'pot luck' with regard to who was your assessor and which cases you saw. The OSCE consists of a number of stations and allows students to be assessed across a wide range of knowledge, skills and attitudes by a range of examiners. This, and the fact that the marks are allocated objectively rather than subjectively, is thought to make the OSCE a more accurate, fair, rigorous and defensible assessment than long or short clinical cases. A well-constructed, well-planned OSCE is therefore thought to offer high validity and moderately good reliability in assessing competence in clinical skills (Newble and Cannon, 1994).

This type of assessment is also used in postgraduate assessments such as the Membership of the Royal College of Physicians (MRCP) Practical Assessment of Clinical Examination Skills (PACES) assessment and PLAB Part II. OSCEs are, and will remain for some time, a part of our professional lives – there is no escaping them!

The OSCE in finals – what?

Most students have had some experience of OSCEs and almost every medical school will use this method of assessment somewhere in their undergraduate course. Many of the OSCEs that students will have been exposed to in earlier years of the curriculum assess simple competencies. Often these are basic practical procedures and tests of examination skills and history-taking skills with more emphasis on technique than findings. At the level of finals, more is expected of students. This is an assessment that aims to judge whether candidates are prepared to take on the role of a health professional. Practising health professionals blend knowledge, skills and attitudes together to diagnose and care for patients, and this is done using problem-solving and clinical reasoning skills (Hartley et al., 2003). This means that the OSCE at finals goes a stage further; these assessments check that candidates have the required knowledge, skills and attitudes and also that they are capable of using these in a targeted and relevant way.

Understanding the OSCE

OSCEs are relatively formulaic and transparent assessments; they are not trying to deceive or pull tricks. The key to doing well in this sort of assessment (apart from just being able in some of the competencies!) is knowing what the assessment is setting out to test, what is likely to be in it, how it is constructed and how it will be marked.

OSCEs are designed to be as **reliable, objective, valid** and **feasible** as possible.

To be **reliable**, a summative OSCE covering a wide curriculum needs more than 20 stations. This means there will be a large number of items in the test. You cannot therefore leave whole chunks of the curriculum out of your revision plans. If you do, you will almost certainly be faced with stations that you haven't the faintest idea how to approach. However, if you spend some time thinking about your *general approach* to certain types of stations, for example communicating in difficult situations or performing joint examinations, and devise some basic principles, no station is likely to faze you completely. The large number of stations means that you can't do perfectly on every station; learn to accept this and you will be able to give every station your best shot. Your medical school may offer sample questions from past papers and you should look at *all* the available examples. This will give you an insight into how the OSCE is marked in your institution, what sort of stations are included, what sort of instructions are given, and how long you have for each type of task. Although there may be a few stations that are brand new each year, many are re-workings of old stations, and being sure you can do well on all past stations you have seen is probably the most important step you can take (other than buying this book of course!).

To aid reliability in an OSCE further, the mark-sheets used must be relatively structured and contain details of how to score or grade students fairly and objectively. There is a variety of mark-sheets used in OSCEs at finals. These fall into two broad groups: mark-sheets with a large series of items which limit markers by only allowing them to indicate if a student has or has not performed a certain activity, and those with broader marking areas and score ranges that allow examiners to use their own judgement with the help of anchor statements. An example of each type of mark-sheet is included at the end of this section. Although these mark-sheets look rather different, well-trained assessors seem to be able to use both relatively objectively. Even in the less itemized type of mark-sheet, anchor statements are often detailed and so assessors are limited to scoring on what they *actually* observed and heard. Although it is difficult to get consensus on what constitutes an excellent or good performance, most practising clinicians are clear about what constitutes a poor performance. So if your assessment uses anchor statements, look carefully at the descriptions of what constitutes a sub-standard performance on each station and use this as a guide to work out what is the very least expected of you for an assessor to pass you.

Finally, if you are aiming for excellent marks, it is worth remembering that ensuring reliability also means that OSCEs often take more than 2 hours per circuit. This means any one examiner may have seen countless students before you. This is a repetitive task, and so it might be a good idea to think about how your performance might stand out from the crowd – just be sure your performance stands out in a good way!

To be **objective**, the cases used in an OSCE need to be reproducible. This is because most institutions will be running the assessment over a considerable number of hours, even days, and often on a number of sites. This need for reproducibility means that any real patients used will have to have relatively common stable conditions and be well enough to sit through hours of examinations. Where role-players (actors or members of the public who have special training to simulate clinical scenarios) are used, the potential for conditions they may be asked to simulate is wider, but even an Oscar winner would have some difficulty simulating a distended tense abdomen! For preparation purposes, it might therefore be sensible to concentrate on common stable conditions for the examination stations and to expect common credible scenarios for the talking stations.

To be **valid**, an assessment has to reflect the breadth of the school's course. This is usually done by 'blueprinting' the assessment. This process ensures that the stations sample across every area of the curriculum to provide an assessment that tests a wide variety of different skills and abilities. Also, a valid assessment will not test outside the defined course objectives, therefore taking time to look at these is worthwhile.

At finals, assessment often goes beyond simply checking whether a student has mastered a clinical skill. Often the station will attempt to assess clinical reasoning by requiring the students to attempt a differential diagnosis. This means that now is a good time to start brushing up on your clinical reasoning skills. The best way to do this is to list common presentations such as chest pain, numbness in the legs etc. Next write down the most common causes for each condition (you may need to check with one of you teachers or in a textbook that you have got these diagnoses correct). Then list the questions and responses that would lead you to choose one diagnosis over another. For example, if the symptom is chest pain and the three most likely diagnoses you have written down are (i) ischaemic, (ii) oesophageal and (iii) muscular pain, positive responses to questions about relation to eating or lying down make it more likely to be oesophageal, whereas positive responses to questions about exertional pain and radiation to the arm make it more likely to be ischaemic. When you are practising histories and examination with each other, stop and reflect regularly: What have I discovered so far? What does it mean with regard to what is going on? What questions or further examination will prove or disprove this theory? With enough practice, these reflective thoughts and hypothesis testing will become a natural part of your clinical acumen.

To be **feasible**, an assessment has to be relatively easy to run. OSCEs are expensive and time consuming, requiring big halls, lots of equipment and plenty of markers. Patients need stable common problems to allow assessment organizers to get enough cases for every candidate to have a similar experience. Very sick patients and examination halls do not go together; there are not the resuscitation facilities available and patient well-being is paramount. This means that rare conditions are unlikely to be tested and the serious conditions represented will be those that are relatively straightforward to simulate (refer back to the paragraph on objectivity in this introductory section). Most OSCEs will use models to assess practical skills for reasons of feasibility. Make sure you are familiar with the skills models held in your clinical skills centre and practise on them – these are likely to be the same models that will be used in the OSCE.

Testing personal and professional development in OSCEs

The General Medical Council (GMC) document *Tomorrow's Doctors* (GMC, 1993, 2003) has had a significant effect on how and what medical schools teach and assess. All schools are required to meet the recommendations in this document. The response of most schools is to have a more integrated curriculum with closer links between the basic and clinical sciences and a greater focus on acquiring professional skills and attitudes. These curriculum changes are matched by changes in what is assessed at finals. For example, some aspects of basic medical science relevant to professional practice, such as using statistical and epidemiological skills to evaluate evidence, are now being tested in finals. Professional skills such as using ethical and legal principles in decision making or making the most of health promotion opportunities are also being tested. Do not leave these areas out of your exam preparation. Also remember that professional attitudes may be tested by observing your behaviour in more complex or demanding stations. Being polite, respectful and non-judgemental with all patients and role-players is essential, as are displaying respect for other members of a team and insight into your own limitations.

How to fail an OSCE

It is possible to be a competent final-year student and fail an OSCE by not knowing what is required of you in the exam, by working hard and not smart. You must, as outlined above, find out exactly what your OSCE entails and prepare for it in an exam-focused way.

You need to convey to your examiners that you are ready to be a doctor, and the way to do this is to act like one! There are therefore some behaviours and tactics that can predictably put you into a 'fail' category. These include lying, being rough with patients or oblivious to their feelings, failing to get consent, being dangerous with equipment, especially sharps, and being cocky or argumentative with the examiner. Conversely, to give yourself the best chance of passing, you should dress professionally and appropriately, appear confident yet not over-confident, be safe, and interact with patients in a caring and pleasant manner. In stressful situations it is sometimes all too easy to pay less attention to these areas in an attempt to get the station completed. To avoid this when you are practising with your colleagues, don't just say 'I would gain the patients consent and ensure comfort' or 'I would dispose of the sharps carefully' – actually **do** the thing. If you practise a behaviour often enough, it will become like second nature. Also remember that the examiner is trying to help you; showing disrespect is guaranteed to loose you valuable marks.

Due to the scale of a finals OSCE, you may be examined at a centre with which you are unfamiliar. Make sure you arrive unflustered by leaving home with lots of extra time and clear instructions of where to report. It is difficult to cope with students who are absent, late arrivals, or those who turn up at the wrong place. Don't start out with the disadvantage of being flustered and looking unprofessional. If you are a borderline candidate, this may be the deciding factor that means you are a fail and not a pass.

OSCEs are daunting and often stations do go disastrously. The last thing you need is for one poor performance to adversely affect the rest of your exam. Difficult though it is, you have to try to collect your thoughts together and be calm for the next station, not allowing yourself to dwell on the disaster of the last.

Finally, those who are experienced in assessment would agree that failing is usually a multi-factorial situation – rarely is the candidate simply not knowledgeable or skilled enough. If you are unwell, emotionally overwrought about the thought of finals, or if something significant is going on in your life that is distracting you from your preparations, speak to your personal tutor or academic advisor as soon as possible and definitely before the assessment. Sharing this information with the right people can only help you in the long run.

Long-case OSCEs

More and more schools are replacing traditional long cases with long-case OSCEs. These are similar in format to other OSCEs but the stations are longer and usually require more complex professional skills. These OSCEs may also include structured orals or vivas, or a variation on the OSCE known as the OSLER (Objective Structured Long Case Examination Record). If your school uses an OSCE format for long cases, it is essential that you get some practice in these sorts of stations with clinicians who are familiar with the format. Be clear with anyone who is helping you to prepare in those final months about exactly *how* you are being assessed. Many clinicians may not be up to date with more recent assessment changes, so if you can give your teacher an example mark-sheet, it will help to focus his/her feedback to you about your performance.

The usefulness of vivas at finals causes fierce debate among medical educators. Structured vivas maintain the strengths of vivas, being useful in assessing all-round knowledge and attitudes, whilst attempting to be more objective and fair. They can still be terrifying assessments, especially as there is likely to be more than one examiner at the station. Get some practice to steady your nerves, and remember that they are designed to test across an area, so don't panic if you cannot answer every question perfectly. Remember, one of their strengths is testing attitudes, so being honest and saying 'I don't know' is important. Also, saying 'I would ask the patient what they wanted' or 'I would consult a senior colleague or the member of the team with the appropriate knowledge or experience' is not a bad answer if you really haven't got a clue.

REFERENCES

General Medical Council. *Tomorrow's Doctors. Recommendations on Undergraduate Medical Education.* London: General Medical Council, 1993, 2003.

Hartley S, Gill D, Walters K, Carter F, Bryant P. *Teaching Medical Students in Primary and Secondary Care – a Resource Book.* Oxford: Oxford University Press, 2003.

Newble D, Cannon R. *A Handbook for Medical Teachers*, 3rd edn. London: Kluwer Academic Publishers, 1994.

EXAMPLE MARK-SHEET

VITAL SIGNS

Examiner: Please confirm the vital signs in this patient before the first candidate. The BP measurement should be within 6 mmHg of your measurement.

Please mark one response for each item like this [_____]

Instructions for candidate

In this station you will be asked to assess and record this patient's vital signs. Please measure the blood pressure, radial pulse rate and rhythm, and respiratory rate of this patient and state your findings to the examiner.

You have 7 minutes

Items	Y	N
1. General approach to patient (courteous, good rapport, ensures comfort etc.)	[ ]	[ ]
Blood Pressure		
2. Chooses correct cuff	[ ]	[ ]
3. Puts cuff on correctly	[ ]	[ ]
4. Feels a pulse and places stethoscope correctly	[ ]	[ ]
5. Inflates cuff, within reason, above pulse pressure	[ ]	[ ]
6. Lowers mercury at appropriate speed	[ ]	[ ]
7. Reports correct blood pressure	[ ]	[ ]
Pulse		
8. Measures rate and rhythm at radial pulse	[ ]	[ ]
9. Reports correct rate	[ ]	[ ]
10. Reports correct rhythm	[ ]	[ ]
Respiratory Rate		
11. Measures rate by observing chest for at least 30 seconds	[ ]	[ ]
12. Reports correct rate	[ ]	[ ]

Global score		
	Clear pass	[ ]
	Borderline pass	[ ]
	Borderline fail	[ ]
	Clear fail	[ ]

EXAMPLE MARK-SHEET

EXAMINATION SKILLS – RHEUMATOID HANDS

Instructions for candidate: Mrs Smith is a 50-year-old lady with rheumatoid arthritis (RA). She complains of painful hands. Please examine her hands. Towards the end of the station I will ask you to present your findings.

Item	Good pass	Pass	Borderline	Fail
1. Appropriate start to the examination	[ ]	[ ]	[ ]	[ ]
	States full name and role, checks preferred form of address, explains nature of examination, gains consent for examination	Introduction of self, gives overview of purpose of examination	Some attempt at introduction, vague description of purpose of examination, makes statement assuming consent	No attempt at introductions, no explanation of purpose of examination, does not gain consent
2. Conducts appropriate examination	[ ]	[ ]	[ ]	[ ]
	Systematic and thorough examination of hands including elbows, watches patients face	Generally appropriate examination	Unsystematic examination, cursory examination of some areas	Unsystematic, misses areas of examination, does not watch patient's face
3. Presents findings of examination	[ ]	[ ]	[ ]	[ ]
	Systematic and accurate summary of findings	Generally accurate summary of findings	Unsystematic description of findings. Some omissions or incorrect findings	Chaotic description, significant omissions or inaccuracies
4. Suggests correct diagnosis (RA)	[ ]	[ ]	[ ]	[ ]
	Correct diagnosis with appropriate weighting of findings in examination to support this	Correct diagnosis	Diagnosis of inflammatory arthritis but not specifically RA	Diagnosis incorrect or no attempt at diagnosis
Global Score	[ ]	[ ]	[ ]	[ ]

SECTION 1:
PRACTICAL SKILLS

SECTION 1: PRACTICAL SKILLS

Practical skills stations are extremely predictable and once mastered are easy to score well on. All you have to do is execute your rehearsed routine, often without facing the added challenge of picking up clinical signs, forming differential diagnoses or interpreting a history. The key to scoring well is to appear slick and fluent, and practice is the only way to achieve this. Some of the practical skills stations will require you to demonstrate the procedures on real patients, and others on mannequins or models.

Initially practical skills are best learnt in the safety of the clinical skills centre, where your mistakes are more easily rectified. These skills should be quickly transferred onto the ward and clinic setting, with doctors and other health professionals supervising and teaching you. Learning them in a real setting gives you an insight into the clinical indications for various procedures and will teach you how the procedures are carried out in practice, which is often different from the 'correct' method you will be taught in a clinical skills teaching session. Practising in a ward setting will also give you the variability and challenges that real patients pose (plastic catheterization models tend not to have enlarged prostate glands!), and therefore help to make you proficient at carrying out practical procedures in preparation for your house jobs. This said, in the run up to your final objective structured clinical examination (OSCE), the clinical skills centre is the most useful place for you to return to practise and rehearse. We would recommend that in the last few weeks before your finals you set aside several sessions to attend the clinical skills centre with two friends to become slick and fluent at the practical skills. Practising with two other people allows one of you, where required, to be the patient and the other to play the role of the examiner, assessing the candidate against the checklists provided in this chapter. Attending a clinical skills centre will allow you to practise the procedures on models, which is often very different from carrying them out on real patients, and also to be in an environment where you can replicate the OSCE setting and rehearse to time. The clinical skills centre at your medical school will provide you with equipment that is actually used in the OSCE so you can familiarize yourself with it in advance of the exam.

Some of the practical skills stations are difficult to complete in the short time given in an OSCE; however, it is surprising just how much you speed up with practice. Once you have mastered each practical skill, your next challenge, which is perhaps just as difficult, is to ensure that you can carry it out in the time allocated in your OSCE. Time is often wasted thinking about what equipment you need, and a useful tip is to memorize lists of equipment for each of the practical skills you may be required to demonstrate. We suggest talking through the procedure as you perform it, drawing the examiner's attention to the fact that you have carried out a particular step and allowing him or her to tick it off on the mark-sheet. You can either talk directly to the examiner or describe what you are doing by way of explanation to the 'patient', if that is required – check with the examiner at the station what he or she would like you to do. If there is a step that you would carry out in reality but are unable to do in the OSCE setting, for example introducing yourself to a mannequin, you should state your intention to do it, allowing the examiner to give you the mark.

In all practical skill stations you should always confirm the 'patient's' identity, checking the wristband on a model and asking a role-player his/her name and date of birth. Ensure that you establish rapport with your 'patient', explain the indication and procedure and seek his/her permission, giving him/her an opportunity to express any concerns. Global marks in practical skills stations are for performing the task correctly and fluently, and for your interaction with the 'patient'. Your examiner may also ask you some questions at the end of the procedure, for example, when assessing nasogastric tube insertion, he/she might ask what you would do if the patient coughed. These questions are to ascertain whether you have in fact performed the task in reality on the wards, to test your wider clinical knowledge, and to give you an opportunity to increase your global score. But, as you can see from the mark-sheets, it is by no means the end of the world if you cannot answer them.

We have included a broad selection of practical skills in this chapter, some of which you will frequently perform as newly qualified doctors, and others which, although more commonly performed by nurses, you ought to know about. You may find that your medical school assesses skills that we have not included, and if this is the case, we suggest devising your own mark-sheets for practice along similar lines to the ones included in this chapter.

BLOOD CULTURES

You are a medical pre-registration house officer (PRHO) on-call and you have been asked to review Mr Whitehurst, who is pyrexial with a temperature of 39 °C following the insertion of a central line. Part of your assessment involves taking blood cultures. Please demonstrate this on the model arm provided.

States intention to introduce self and confirm patient's name and date of birth
States intention to explain the need for obtaining blood cultures and the procedure, and to seek the patient's permission
Selects appropriate equipment for the test (green needle/s, 10/20 mL syringe, blood culture bottle/s, alcohol wipes, tourniquet, gloves and cotton swabs)
Washes hands and puts on gloves
Applies tourniquet to model arm and selects a vein
Cleans the skin using alcohol swabs
Retracts vein to stabilize it and inserts needle into the vein using aseptic technique
Ensures that adequate blood sample has been withdrawn (5–10 mL is required per bottle)
Releases tourniquet and withdraws needle, whilst achieving haemostasis with a cotton swab
Removes caps from blood culture bottles and cleans tops with alcohol wipes
Fills each blood culture bottle with the correct volume of blood, filling the anaerobic bottle first
Discards needle and syringe safely
Labels each bottle appropriately
Completes the correct request form with necessary clinical information
Documents taking of blood cultures in the notes

 ## Global marks

Examiner global rating

KEY TIPS

Depending on which hospital/medical school you are at, you will be required to fill either one or two (aerobic and anaerobic) blood culture bottles.

There are two schools of thought when it comes to changing to a sterile needle after blood has been drawn, and prior to filling the blood culture bottles. The reason is that although changing the needle reduces the risk of contaminating the sample with skin flora, it also increases the chance of needlestick injury. It is worth checking with your medical school whether or not they prefer the needle to be replaced with a sterile one.

Remember that although not a sterile procedure, you do need to be as aseptic as possible in order to reduce contamination of the culture medium. So, clean the selected venepuncture site with plenty of alcohol wipes from the centre outwards, allow the skin to dry before puncture, and once the site is cleaned do not palpate the vein again!

BASIC LIFE SUPPORT (BLS)

You are called to the ward to assess a collapsed patient. Please demonstrate basic life support on the mannequin provided.

Demonstrates a safe approach (i.e. does not pose hazard to self or 'patient')

Approaches the 'patient' and checks for responsiveness using verbal and physical stimulation

If no response, shouts for help

Checks in the mouth for foreign objects and removes any visible obstruction

Opens the 'patient's' airway using either a jaw thrust technique or head tilt – chin lift as appropriate

Checks for signs of breathing for 10 seconds (looks, listens and feels)

If the 'patient' is not breathing, goes to get help, and ensures a cardiac arrest call has been put out

Performs two effective rescue breaths using a pocket-mask

Checks for signs of a circulation for 10 seconds

If no carotid pulse, performs 15 chest compressions using the correct technique

Continues resuscitation using the correct ratio of two breaths to 15 chest compressions until help arrives

 ## Global marks

Examiner global rating

KEY TIPS ━●

You are expected to know advanced life support (ALS) prior to becoming a PRHO, and most medical schools normally run a compulsory course for all students to attend. You will probably not be asked to perform ALS in the OSCE due to the practical difficulties of it, but what you will be required to do is perform BLS and to answer questions with regard to ALS, perhaps even demonstrating aspects of it on a mannequin. You should know how to connect the mannequin to a cardiac monitor and where to place the paddles, and you should be able to talk through defibrillation. You should recognize rhythm strips for supraventricular tachycardia, ventricular tachycardia, ventricular fibrillation and asystole, and know the principles of electro-mechanical dissociation. You will be expected to know the drug doses that form part of the ALS algorithm.

We recommend that that you learn the most current algorithms for BLS and ALS, which can be found on the UK Resuscitation Council website (www.resus.org.uk).

MALE CATHETERIZATION

As a PRHO you will be expected to catheterize male patients when required. Please demonstrate your catheterization skills on the mannequin provided.

States intention to introduce self and confirm patient's name and date of birth
States intention to explain the need for catheterization and the procedure, and to seek the patient's permission
Cleans catheterization trolley
Arranges all the equipment required using sterile technique where appropriate
States that would normally position patient flat on the bed exposing the groin area
Washes hands and puts on sterile gloves
Uses one hand to hold the penis with sterile swabs and cleans the penis, using the other hand, with a 'no touch' technique
Covers the area with sterile towels, leaving the penis exposed
States intention to retract the foreskin if one is present
Inserts lignocaine gel and states that would normally allow a few minutes for it to work
Inserts the catheter correctly, using a sterile technique and negotiating the prostate gland
States intention to ensure that urine is draining into a sterile receptacle
Inflates the cuff with the correct volume of sterile water for injection
Withdraws the catheter until resistance is felt
Connects the catheter to the catheter bag
States intention to replace the foreskin if one is present
States intention to ensure that patient has been re-clothed, and all equipment has been tidied away
Records in the medical notes the time of catheter insertion, type and size of catheter inserted, volume of water used to inflate the cuff, and residual volume of urine

Global marks

Examiner global rating

KEY TIPS ⚯

This is a difficult station to complete in a short period of time, and our only advice is that practice (in your clinical skills centre, with the equipment you are likely to be given in the OSCE) makes perfect!

You will find it easy to remember the equipment you need if you remember that there are eight items, and these are:

12 or 14 gauge male catheter
sterile catheter pack
sterile gloves (know your size!)
10 mL syringe
sterile water for injection
lignocaine gel in a pre-filled syringe
sterile saline for cleaning
catheter bag.

Check the expiry date of the catheter and the volume of water required to inflate the catheter cuff before you open the catheter out onto the sterile field. Some catheters come with a pre-filled syringe of sterile water for inflating the cuff, but if this is not the case, prepare one yourself and leave it outside the sterile field before putting on sterile gloves. Also, before putting on sterile gloves, you should remember to pour saline for cleaning into the container provided in the catheter pack. If at any stage you lose your sterility, state your intention to wash your hands and put on a new pair of sterile gloves.

It is useful to explain to the examiner what you are doing at each stage of the procedure; this enables him/her to follow your steps even if it is not obvious and to give you as many of the marks opposite as possible. If you encounter difficulties inserting the actual catheter, state to the examiner that you would lower the penis to help negotiate the prostate gland and, if this fails, retry with a larger gauge catheter before asking for senior help.

INTRAVENOUS INJECTION

You are a PRHO on-call. Mrs White has a chest infection and the nurse looking after her has asked you to administer her intravenous (i.v.) co-amoxiclav as she is unable to. Please demonstrate this skill using the model arm provided.

States intention to introduce self and confirm patient's name and date of birth
States intention to explain the need for i.v. antibiotics and the procedure, and to seek permission
States intention to check allergy status with patient and as documented on drug chart and patient's wristband
Checks vial of co-amoxiclav for dose and expiry date
States that would double-check drug name, dose and expiry with another member of medical or nursing staff
Refers to the *British National Formulary* (BNF) for correct administration instructions
Washes hands and wears gloves
Applies tourniquet to model arm and selects a suitable vein
Cleans skin with an alcohol swab
Retracts skin to stabilize the vein and inserts cannula until flashback seen
Correctly advances cannula over needle, withdrawing needle partially to secure intravenous access
Releases tourniquet, completely withdraws the needle and caps the end of the cannula
Disposes of the needle safely
Secures cannula in place
Reconstitutes drug using correct volume of suitable diluent as per BNF instructions
Draws reconstituted drug into syringe, administers via cannula at correct speed as per BNF instructions
Disposes of needle and drug ampoule safely
Signs and records time of administration on drug chart, asking the other health professional who checked the drugs to sign the chart as well

 ## Global marks

Examiner global rating

KEY TIPS ⚊●

Before administering an intravenous drug you should always refer to the BNF to check what form the drug comes in, whether it needs reconstituting and, if so, how much and what diluent to use, and to check the speed of administration. Remember to check with the patient and with his/her drug chart and wristband for any allergies. Most commonly, intravenous drugs are administered via an i.v. line, be it a peripheral or a central line; however, you may be asked to administer an i.v. drug using only a needle and a syringe. Essentially the same principles as those outlined opposite apply; however, any differences are highlighted in the mark scheme that follows. The first six steps are identical to those opposite.

Washes hands and wears gloves
Reconstitutes drug using correct volume of suitable diluent as per BNF instructions
Draws reconstituted drug into syringe
Disposes of ampoule safely
Applies tourniquet to model arm and selects a suitable vein
Cleans skin with an alcohol wipe
Retracts skin to stabilize the vein and inserts green needle and prepared syringe into vein until flashback seen
Releases tourniquet
Administers drug at correct speed as per BNF instructions
Withdraws needle and achieves haemostasis by applying pressure over puncture site using a cotton swab
Disposes of needle safely
Signs and records time of administration on drug chart asking the other health professional who checked the drugs to sign the chart as well

Reconstituting powdered drugs is not as straightforward as it might seem, and if you have not done it before, ask a nurse to show you how.

OXYGEN THERAPY

You are a medical PRHO and your firm is on-take. Mr Williams is an 80-year-old gentleman with known chronic obstructive pulmonary disease (COPD) who has presented to the accident and emergency department (A&E) short of breath. Please manage his oxygen therapy appropriately, explaining to the examiner as you go along.

Introduces self and confirms patient's name and date of birth
Checks patient's oxygen saturation using pulse oximetry
Comments on adequacy of oxygen saturation
Offers arterial blood gas sampling
Correctly interprets blood gas results provided by the examiner
States need for oxygen therapy
Chooses a fixed-performance mask and valve to deliver 24 per cent oxygen
Correctly applies mask to patient, tightening the elastic straps and ensuring a good fit
Turns on oxygen at correct flow rate to deliver 24 per cent
States intention to repeat arterial blood gas sampling after half an hour
Correctly interprets second blood gas results provided by the examiner
Changes concentration of oxygen appropriately
Prescribes oxygen on treatment chart

Global marks

Examiner global rating

KEY TIPS ⊸●

This station is testing your ability to manage oxygen therapy for a COPD patient appropriately, a common encounter both in A&E and on the wards. Oxygen therapy for COPD patients can be very delicate, and you must always consider that the patient may be reliant on a hypoxic drive and will therefore begin to retain carbon dioxide if over-oxygenated.

It is important to use a fixed-performance mask in COPD, so that you know exactly how much oxygen the patient is receiving when you are interpreting the results of arterial blood gases. It is worth becoming familiar with different oxygen masks, and practising connecting the tubing to the oxygen supply. A&E is a good place to practise oxygen therapy, and a session with a respiratory nurse specialist will give you an opportunity to see and learn about different masks.

In the scenario opposite, the first arterial blood gas will probably show a low pO_2 and a normal or low pCO_2. With a COPD patient, unless he or she is very hypoxic, you should commence oxygen therapy at 24 per cent, rechecking the arterial blood gas 30 minutes later. The second arterial blood gas may reveal normal gases, in which case you would state to the examiner that you would like to continue oxygen therapy at 24 per cent. Or it may reveal that the patient remains hypoxic, without significant carbon dioxide retention, in which case you would change the valve and flow rate to deliver 28 per cent, rechecking the arterial blood gas after a further 30 minutes. If your 'patient' is retaining carbon dioxide, you should state to the examiner that you would discuss the results with your senior, to consider alternative methods of respiratory support (e.g. non-invasive positive pressure ventilation).

In the scenario opposite you were informed that the patient had COPD; however, with an elderly patient who has been or is a smoker, you should always be cautious with oxygen therapy, as he/she may have an element of COPD.

NASOGASTRIC TUBE INSERTION

As a PRHO you will be expected to insert nasogastric (NG) tubes into patients when a nurse is unable to. Please demonstrate your NG insertion skills on the mannequin provided. In this case you are inserting a NG tube as part of the management of gastrointestinal obstruction.

States intention to introduce self and confirm patient's name and date of birth
States intention to explain the need for a NG tube and the procedure, and to seek permission
States that the patient should be sitting upright
Gathers correct equipment and sets up a non-sterile trolley
Washes hands and puts on non-sterile gloves
Correctly measures the length of tube to be inserted
States intention to ask the patient which nostril he/she would prefer the tube to be inserted into
States intention to give the patient a glass of water (if clinically appropriate) and ask him/her to hold the water in his/her mouth ready to swallow when instructed to do so
Lubricates tube using jelly and inserts into nostril and nasopharynx
States intention to encourage the patient to swallow the water when insertion feels uncomfortable (if clinically appropriate)
Inserts nasogastric tube to desired length
Checks that the tube is correctly placed in the stomach
Tapes the tube to the 'patient's' nose, and connects it to a dependent catheter bag

Global marks

Examiner global rating

KEY TIPS ⚊●

There are two types of NG tube: wide bore and narrow bore. Wide-bore tubes are used before and after gastrointestinal surgery, in intestinal obstruction, and to prevent aspiration of intestinal contents into the lungs. Narrow-bore tubes are used for enteric feeding. NG tubes come in different sizes and, as a general rule, a 12-gauge tube will be appropriate for most patients. When inserting a NG tube you will require the following equipment:

NG tube
non-sterile gloves
a glass of water (if appropriate)
lubricating jelly
a vomit bowl
tape
a 20 mL syringe if inserting a wide-bore tube
a stethoscope or pH paper if inserting a wide-bore tube
catheter bag.

First, measure the length of tube that will need to be inserted by placing the tip of the tube at the mannequin's nostril, stretching it across the face to the ear and then to two finger breadths above the umbilicus. To insert the tube, you initially insert upwards along the base of the nasal passage into the nasopharynx, and then advance the tube towards the occiput. Insertion of a NG tube is not a painful procedure but is uncomfortable and can induce gagging when the tube hits the nasopharynx. If clinically appropriate, patients are asked to swallow the water they are holding in their mouths as soon as they feel the sensation to gag. This closes off the epiglottis, making it less likely that the tube will end up in a bronchus. If patients cough, the tube is withdrawn slightly, allowing them to recover before trying to advance it again. From time to time, patients are asked to open their mouths to check that the tube is actually being advanced into the pharynx and oesophagus and not just coiling up inside the mouth!

There are three ways of checking that a wide-bore tube is inside the stomach. First, you can aspirate stomach contents and test the aspirate against pH paper – stomach contents are acidic. The second method is to connect the tube to a 20 mL syringe that is full of air, and to inject a fast gush of air into the tube whilst listening over the epigastrium with a stethoscope for the air gush. Finally, if you have any doubts, you can always request a chest X-ray to check that the tip of the tube is indeed below the diaphragm. A narrow-bore tube is too narrow to aspirate from, and to inject a fast gush of air into. Therefore you will need to request a chest X-ray to ensure that the tube is correctly placed and this should be done before the guide-wire, which is radio-opaque, is removed.

Insertion of NG tubes is best learnt under the instruction of a nurse on a surgical ward, where it is commonly performed.

CONFIRMING A DEATH

You are a medical PRHO doing a ward on-call. You have been bleeped by the nursing staff to confirm the expected death of a patient. Please demonstrate how you would confirm that a patient was dead using the mannequin provided, and explain your actions to the examiner as you go along.

States intention to ask the nurse for a brief history of the background to the death and to confirm that the patient was not for resuscitation
States intention to read the patient's medical notes
Confirms the identity of the 'patient' by checking the wristband
Exposes the 'patient' adequately and observes, commenting on the absence of respiratory movements
Palpates for a carotid pulse on both sides
Palpates for both radial pulses
Palpates for both femoral pulses
Auscultates over the praecordium for 1 minute, commenting on the absence of heart sounds
Auscultates over the chest for 3 minutes, commenting on the absence of breath sounds
Inspects the eyes with a pen torch for fixed and dilated pupils
Examines the fundi with an ophthalmoscope for segmentation of the retinal columns
Washes hands
Documents the findings in the medical notes, stating the date and time of death
Signs and prints name and designation in the medical notes
States intention to ask the nurse to contact the deceased's next of kin

Global marks

Examiner global rating

KEY TIPS

Below is an example of how a death is documented in the medical notes.

29/1/04
04.00 hours
PRHO ON-CALL
Asked to confirm expected death by nursing staff. Medical notes reviewed and noted that patient was not for resuscitation and for supportive care only, with imminent death expected.
No cardiovascular effort.
No respiratory effort.
Pupils fixed and dilated.
Segmentation of retinal columns on fundoscopic examination.
Date and time of death: 29/1/04, 03.30 hours.
Rest in peace.

DAVIES, PRHO bleep 2440

As part of this station you may be asked questions about death certification – it is worth becoming familiar with how to complete death certificates, and knowing when post-mortem examination may be required.

RECORDING AN ELECTROCARDIOGRAM

Please record an electrocardiogram (ECG) for Mr Hughes.

Introduces self and confirms patient's name and date of birth
Explains the need for an ECG and the procedure, and seeks permission
Positions and exposes the patient adequately
Applies stickers in the correct positions on the chest wall and limbs, ensuring good skin contact
Attaches ECG leads to the stickers correctly
Records a technically sound ECG
Labels ECG correctly
Removes stickers from the patient and ensures that the patient is made comfortable
Cleans hands by washing or using alcohol gel
Interprets ECG correctly
States intention to file ECG in medical notes

Global marks

Examiner global rating

KEY TIPS ⚊●

For recording an ECG, your patient should be rested and sitting at 45° with his/her chest, arms and ankles exposed. The positions of the leads are:

V1 – 4th intercostal space to the right of the sternum
V2 – 4th intercostal space to the left of the sternum
V3 – in the middle of V2 and V4
V4 – 5th intercostal space in the midclavicular line
V5 – in the same horizontal plane as V4 but in the anterior axillary line
V6 – in the same horizontal plane as V4 and V5 but in the midaxillary line
The limb leads are placed on the shoulders and thighs or ankles.

In order to achieve a clear tracing, you should instruct your patient to remain very still. A technically sound ECG is one in which all 12 leads have recorded and the tracing is clear and reliable for interpretation. Check that your ECG is technically sound before removing the stickers from your patient.

You should be able to recognize common ECG abnormalities such as ST elevation, presence of Q waves, ST depression, T wave inversion or peaking, bundle branch block and arrhythmias.

DOPPLER MEASUREMENT OF ANKLE–BRACHIAL PRESSURE INDEX

You are a surgical PRHO on a vascular firm and you have been asked to measure the ankle–brachial pressure index (ABPI) in Mr Campbell's right leg.

Introduces self and confirms patient's name and date of birth

Explains the need for measuring the ABPI and the procedure, and seeks permission

Positions and exposes the patient adequately

Locates the brachial pulse of either arm and measures the brachial systolic pressure using the hand-held Doppler

States intention to measure the brachial systolic pressure in the other arm and to use the higher of the two readings to calculate the ABPI

Locates the posterior tibial pulse in the right leg and measures the posterior tibial systolic pressure using the hand-held Doppler

Locates the dorsalis pedis pulse in the right leg and measures the dorsalis pedis systolic pressure using the hand-held Doppler

Calculates the ABPI for the dorsalis pedis and posterior tibial pulses

Interprets results correctly

Ensures that patient is made comfortable

Cleans hands by washing or using alcohol gel

Explains results to patient appropriately

 ## Global marks

Examiner global rating

KEY TIPS ⟜●

This is a difficult skill to demonstrate fluently and in the short time available for an OSCE station. If the time in your OSCE is short, you will probably only be expected to measure the ABPI in one leg, and you can save time by stating that you would measure the brachial systolic pressure in both arms and simply demonstrate it in one. It is the higher of the two brachial systolic pressure readings that is used to calculate the ABPI. You need to be familiar with the anatomical landmarks of the brachial, dorsalis pedis and posterior tibial pulses and with palpating pulses.

Your patient should be lying at 45° with his/her sleeves and trousers rolled up. To measure the brachial systolic pressure, place the cuff above the elbow and palpate the pulse to locate where it is maximally felt, placing a small amount of conductive jelly at this site. Hold the Doppler probe at 45° to the skin and apply gentle pressure without occluding the artery to achieve the best possible signal. Then inflate the cuff until the signal is abolished, deflate it slowly and record the pressure at which the signal is again audible. Recording the posterior tibial and dorsalis pedis systolic pressures is similar, but the cuff is applied mid-calf, and you should explain to the patient that it might feel uncomfortable. Sometimes it is difficult to locate the foot pulses by palpation or with the Doppler probe and if, for example, the posterior tibial pulse is proving difficult, move on to the dorsalis pedis quickly and return to the posterior tibial if time permits.

The ABPI for the posterior tibial pulse is *posterior tibial systolic pressure/highest brachial systolic pressure*. The ABPI for the dorsalis pedis pulse is *dorsalis pedis systolic pressure/highest brachial systolic pressure*. An ABPI of 1–1.2 is normal, 0.4–0.9 represents claudication and an ABPI of less than 0.4 is indicative of critical ischaemia.

The best place to become proficient at measuring ABPIs is in a vascular outpatient clinic.

SETTING UP A SYRINGE DRIVER

You are required to set up a subcutaneous syringe driver with 15 mg of diamorphine and 10 mg of midazolam for Mrs Black, who is on a terminal care pathway for oesophageal cancer. Please make the total volume up to 10 mL, to run over 24 hours.

States intention to introduce self and confirm patient's name and date of birth
States intention to explain the need for setting up a syringe driver and the procedure, and to seek permission (if appropriate)
Selects the correct syringe driver (Graseby MS 26, or equivalent)
Checks that the battery is in place and the device functioning
Selects a 10 mL Luer-lock syringe
Selects the correct subcutaneous giving set
Checks the identity of the patient against the prescription chart
Checks the doses and expiry dates for midazolam and diamorphine on the vials
Asks a colleague (nurse or doctor) to confirm the names, doses and expiry dates of the drugs selected
Wears gloves
Draws up the correct doses of the drugs into the syringe
Draws up the correct diluent to make a total volume of 10 mL and shakes syringe with needle capped to mix
Attaches giving set to the syringe and runs the infusion through it
Measures the length in millimetres of the 10 mL volume and correctly calculates the rate of the infusion
Labels the syringe with the correct information
Fits the syringe correctly into the syringe driver
Sets the syringe driver to the rate required
Places the giving set subcutaneously and starts the infusion (a mannequin may be used)
Signs the drug chart appropriately, asking the other health professional who checked the drugs to sign the chart as well

Global marks

Examiner global rating

KEY TIPS 🔑

Although not a skill commonly performed by doctors, your medical school may require that you know how to set up a syringe driver for your final OSCE. There are essentially two different types of syringe driver. First there is the 50 mL syringe pump, which is commonly used for heparin, insulin and glyceryl trinitrate infusions, and for epidural and patient-controlled analgesia pumps. The second type, commonly a Graseby syringe driver, fits a 10 mL or 20 mL syringe, depending on the volume of diluent required, and is most often used in palliative care. This station is written for a Graseby syringe driver, but you could adapt the mark-sheet for its equivalent, or the larger syringe pump if these are the types your medical school requires you to know about.

There are two types of Graseby syringe driver: the blue Graseby MS 16A is designed to be set at an hourly rate and the green Graseby MS 26 is designed to be set at a 12, 24 or 48 hourly rate. Just as for the intravenous drug injection station, you should check the names, doses and expiry dates of the drugs you are going to administer alone and with a colleague. You also need to check which diluent should be used, information that can be found in the BNF.

The syringe should be labelled with the following information:

patient's name, date of birth and hospital number
date and time when the infusion was made up
doses and names of the drugs
diluent used and its volume
rate at which the syringe driver has been set
your name.

To calculate the rate, you measure the length in millimetres that the total volume in the syringe occupies. For the Graseby 16A, divide the length in millimetres by the number of hours over which the infusion should be given. For the Graseby MS26, divide the length in millimetres by the number of days over which the infusion should be given.

Subcutaneous infusion sites are anteriorly in the upper arms and thighs, and in the anterior chest and abdominal wall, and a butterfly needle is used.

Setting up syringe drivers is a skill best learnt under the guidance of nursing staff, and they will be able to teach you about both the 50 mL syringe pump and the smaller Graseby syringe driver.

BLOOD TRANSFUSION

You are a PRHO on-call. Mr Goldberg is an elderly gentleman who had a significant episode of rectal bleeding earlier, dropping his haemoglobin to 7.0 g/dL. As the only free member of staff on the ward, you are administering his first unit of blood. Please demonstrate this using the model arm provided.

States intention to introduce self and confirm patient's name and date of birth
States intention to explain the need for a blood transfusion and the procedure, and to seek the patient's permission
Ensures that baseline observations have been recorded
Washes hands and wears gloves
Applies tourniquet to model arm and selects a suitable vein
Cleans skin with an alcohol wipe
Retracts skin to stabilize the vein and inserts appropriate sized cannula until flashback seen
Correctly advances cannula over needle, withdrawing needle partially to secure intravenous access
Releases tourniquet, completely withdraws the needle and caps the end of the cannula
Disposes of the needle safely
Secures cannula in place
Chooses correct i.v. administration set and primes with normal saline
Runs normal saline through the cannula
Checks the patient's hospital number, name, date of birth and blood group as labelled on the unit of blood against the accompanying sheet from the transfusion laboratory with a qualified health professional (nurse/doctor)
Checks the hospital number, date of birth and name as labelled on the unit of blood with the 'patient's' wristband, and states intention to check also with the patient himself
Documents the serial number of the unit of blood on the drug chart and signs it, asking the other health professional who checked the blood to sign the chart as well
Correctly changes the bag of saline to blood
Commences the blood infusion at the rate prescribed on the chart
Ensures that appropriate observations for adverse reactions will be commenced by the nursing staff

Global marks

Examiner global rating

KEY TIPS 🔑

Giving a blood transfusion is essentially a three-part process: (i) a cross-match sample needs to be taken and the blood prescribed on the drug chart (not described opposite), (ii) a cannula needs to be inserted, and (iii) the units of blood are administered. You may not be required to do all three in a short OSCE station – read the instructions carefully!

Blood is prescribed on the intravenous infusion section of most charts; however, there may be a separate section for blood transfusion. Be familiar with the drug charts used at your university hospital, as these are probably the charts that will be used in the OSCE. Blood needs to be prescribed on the chart before a nurse or healthcare assistant is able to collect the blood from the transfusion laboratory. Each unit is prescribed separately and if the patient is elderly or has a history of heart failure, you should also prescribe 20 mg of frusemide with alternate units of blood. This is prescribed either orally or intravenously on the 'once only' section of the chart, and it is your responsibility to ensure that the nurse knows it is required. In the non-acute setting, each unit is usually prescribed to be given over a period of 4 hours.

When blood arrives from the transfusion laboratory, each unit is supplied with an information sheet detailing the patient's hospital number, date of birth, name and blood type. These details must be checked against the label on the unit of blood to ensure that it is the correct blood for that patient. In addition, you must check the patient's identification details, both with the patient and with his or her wristband, to ensure that you are administering blood to the correct patient. A green cannula would be adequate for non-acute transfusion but if the blood is required quickly, you should secure a 16G (grey) cannula in the antecubital fossa. Blood giving sets have a double barrel with a filter, and look quite different from the giving sets used for normal i.v. administration.

Transfusion reactions are not uncommon and it is important to have baseline observations (pulse rate, blood pressure and temperature) recorded prior to the transfusion as a reference. Once the transfusion has commenced, observations should take place at 0, 15 and 30 minutes and then hourly; nursing staff should also be observing for shortness of breath, urticaria and signs of anaphylaxis. There are four acute types of transfusion reaction – ABO incompatibility, febrile reaction, anaphylactic reaction and urticarial reaction – and you might be asked about how these are managed. With ABO incompatibility, your patient may become hypotensive and dyspnoeic and develop intravascular haemorrhage and you must stop the transfusion. In a febrile reaction, try slowing the transfusion and administering paracetamol. An anaphylactic reaction requires you to stop the transfusion immediately and manage the patient as for anaphylactic shock. If an urticarial rash develops, try slowing the transfusion and administering intravenous chlopheniramine. If you stop an infusion, you must keep the bag and the giving set and send them to the laboratory for analysis, flushing the cannula to ensure that intravenous access remains patent.

SECTION 2: EXAMINATION

SECTION 2: EXAMINATION

Examination stations will form a significant part of your final objective structured clinical examination (OSCE), and should be well rehearsed as they tend to be fairly predictable and, once mastered, easy to score good marks on. OSCE-style examination stations are not dissimilar to traditional short-cases, and essentially what will please the examiner is the same: a fluent and competent examination accompanied by a succinct and confident presentation of your findings, differential diagnoses and investigation plan. Easier said then done! You must jump the hurdle of being embarrassed to perform examinations in front of people early on in your clinical career, be they your peers or teachers, enabling you to perfect your technique.

Attending outpatient clinics is a great way to learn and practise examinations, as you have a good chance of seeing clinical signs, and you will be able to repeat a single examination several times during the course of a session. You will also be able to practise the examinations that prove more difficult on the ward, for example examination of the nose in an ear, nose and throat (ENT) clinic, or a venous examination in a vascular clinic. To maximize your session in clinic, explain to the consultant that you would like to practise examining and presenting your findings formally from the point of view of finals, and you may even want to hand him or her a mark-sheet against which to assess you. Practising in small groups using each other as patients is useful; so, too, is finding patients on the ward with clinical signs who do not mind being examined. A good way to locate such patients is to bleep the junior doctors in your hospital on a regular basis and ask them if they have any patients with clinical signs who would be good to examine. In the run up to your final OSCE, whenever you practise an examination you should always ensure that you have an 'examiner' who can assess you. Practise it to time, present your findings to your 'examiner', suggest differential diagnoses and ask for feedback. If you have a talkative patient, explain to him/her that you are rehearsing for an exam and need to practise timing your examination, but that you will chat to them once you have finished.

You can also prepare a list of differential diagnoses for each type of examination, which is essentially a list of common chest cases for the chest examination station, abdominal cases for the abdominal examination and so on. Whilst conducting each examination, you should be working through the list in your mind, thinking about which case you have been given and then looking carefully for the expected clinical signs. We have assisted you somewhat in this by listing the common OSCE scenarios for each type of examination. OSCE cases are limited to chronic, stable and common conditions; patients are booked for the OSCE months in advance.

Generally, in all examination stations, confirm the patient's name and age. Explain to the patient what examination you would like to perform and seek his/her permission. Politely ask your patient if he/she would mind removing items of clothing, and maintain his/her dignity by covering up parts you do not need to expose all the time. If relevant and permitted, start with a very brief history to help focus your examination and differential diagnoses; check whether a history is required in your school and how detailed it should be. If in your school the focus is simply on conducting the examination, the only question you should ask every time is 'Before I begin, does it hurt anywhere?' It is always worth starting the examination by standing at the end of the bed and taking in the scene, for example sputum pots and nebulizer masks, and inspecting your patient for any obvious clinical signs, such as surgical scars.

It cannot be stressed just how important a fluent, confident and succinct presentation of your findings and differential diagnoses is. Not only are specific marks allocated for it, but you will also impress your examiner and, if applicable, improve your global score. You will need to build the presentation into your examination, and a reasonable division of time in a 7-minute station would be to spend 5 minutes actually carrying out the examination and 2 minutes on the presentation. There are two ways of approaching this. You can either perform the examination in silence and present all your findings at the end, or you can talk through the examination, presenting as you go along with a summary at the end. We feel that the latter approach will be more successful for most candidates, as you will be drawing the examiner's attention to the fact that you have performed a particular step in the examination, allowing him or her to tick it off on the mark-sheet. However, the pitfall with this method is that you need to be very sure of your clinical signs; you will not have the benefit of the full picture before you begin to describe them. If you are not sure whether a clinical sign is indeed present, leave commenting on it until later when you have had a chance to think about it. For most students this is most likely to occur with the cardiovascular examination, and for this station you may benefit from presenting your findings at the end, giving you an opportunity to modify what you say in light of your differential diagnoses! You should, however, describe to the examiner what you are doing at each stage of the examination – the examiner might have seen countless students before you and his/her concentration may be waning.

Below is a commentary of an abdominal examination station, giving you an idea of how to present an examination.

To the patient: Hello, I'm Sarah, a final year medical student. I've been asked to examine your abdomen. Is that okay with you?

Before we continue, I'd just like to confirm your name and age.

Would you mind taking off your shirt for this examination?

I'd like you to be lying flat, with one pillow, so can I take these pillows away? Are you comfortable?

Before we go any further Mrs Jones, do you have any pain anywhere?

To the examiner: Ideally, I would like to expose Mrs Jones's groin, but for the purposes of this examination I will only expose the abdomen.

On general inspection Mrs Jones looks well, there is no jaundice or obvious weight loss.

Her hands are warm and well-perfused and there is no clubbing, leuconychia, palmar erythema or Dupuytren's contracture.

There is no liver flap present.

I can see an arterio-venous (A-V) fistula on her right arm.

Her sclera are not jaundiced, and she is not clinically anaemic.

She is well hydrated and not cyanosed.

On palpation of her cervical lymph nodes, none is enlarged. I was especially feeling for Virchow's node.

There are no spider naevi present on either the front or the back of her thorax.

Moving to her abdomen, on inspection I can see a surgical scar in her right loin. There is nothing else of note.

She is not tender on palpation and her abdomen is soft.

I can feel a smooth and well-defined mass in the right iliac fossa.

There is no hepatomegaly or splenomegaly.

The kidneys are not ballotable.

I cannot feel the abdominal aorta and the bladder is not distended.

On auscultation, she has normal bowel sounds.

There are no hernias in the groins.

I would normally perform a digital rectal examination *(the examiner will tell you that this is not necessary)*.

In summary, this is Mrs Jones, a 49-year-old lady, and I have just examined her abdomen. The positive findings are an A-V fistula on the right arm, a surgical scar in the right loin suggestive of nephrectomy, and a mass in the right iliac fossa. This mass is smooth and well defined. It is non-pulsatile, and not tender. Mrs Jones could have a transplanted kidney on the right side following right-sided kidney failure, dialysis and nephrectomy. To investigate the mass further, I would like initially to request an ultrasound scan of the lower abdomen.

Giving a fluent presentation is hard. Again, our only advice is that practice makes perfect! Whilst presenting, appear confident and sure of your clinical findings (remember, you are trying to convey that you can behave like a doctor and inspire confidence in your patients) and state them in the affirmative. This means saying 'There is no clubbing', not 'I am looking for clubbing, and I don't think that there is any'. It is useful to rehearse a model presentation for each type of examination so that in the OSCE your presentation as well as examination will flow easily, and all you will need to do is substitute into your model any clinical findings and think about differential diagnoses.

For examination stations, the global score, if applicable, is made up of five components. The examiner will be looking for a slick examination; you should look as though you have done it on countless previous occasions. The examiner will be assessing your competence at picking up clinical signs, which is a reflection of your exposure to clinical medicine. He/she will mark you well if your presentation and summarization skills are confident and succinct, and will be looking for correct interpretation of clinical signs, a sensible differential diagnosis and investigation plan. Finally, your interaction and rapport with the patient are important and will be rewarded. This may seem like a daunting combination of skills to demonstrate, but the most important are actually performing the examination well and appearing confident. Don't be too concerned if you are not sure of the clinical findings and differential diagnoses.

Some scenarios in which it may be difficult to know exactly how to conduct the examination and what to include in a short OSCE station – such as examination of the back or lymph nodes – are described in some detail. Others are fairly standard examinations, which you will find well described in other textbooks and will probably already be familiar with. These are not explained in as much detail.

HIP JOINT

Mrs Perrera is an 80-year-old lady complaining of pain in her right hip. Please take a very short history about the pain, perform an appropriate examination and present your findings to the examiner.

Makes appropriate introduction of self and seeks permission to take a history and examine
Confirms patient's name and age

 ## History

Enquires about the site of the pain
Enquires about the degree of pain
Enquires about mobility, walking aids and lifestyle implications
Asks if patient is currently in pain

 ## Look

Ensures patient is in supine position with legs fully exposed
Inspects both legs for deformities
Inspects both legs for muscle wasting and surgical scars

 ## Feel

Palpates both legs for temperature and greater trochanteric tenderness
Assesses for leg length inequality (offers measurement of true and apparent leg lengths)
Measures fixed flexion deformity (looks at the angle between the bed and the thigh or performs Thomas' test)

 ## Move

Assesses hip flexion
Assesses hip internal rotation
Assesses hip external rotation
Assesses hip adduction
Assesses hip abduction
Checks for any distal neurovascular deficit (palpates right pedal pulses and briefly assesses for motor and sensory function of right foot)
Performs Trendelenburg test
Assesses gait

Cleans hands by washing or using alcohol gel

 ## Global marks

Fluency of examination
Competence in presenting findings, summarizing and forming differential diagnosis

KEY TIPS —●

In a history, remember to establish where the pain is maximally felt and where it radiates to. Ask specifically about knee pain, as primary hip disorders may present with isolated knee pain. You should ask about stiffness, and whether it is related to the time of day, movement or staying still.

Examining the hip is physically challenging so will require practice on willing friends if you are to appear fluent. Start the examination with your patient lying down and, to inspect for leg length inequality, ensure that the anterior superior iliac spines (ASISs) are aligned, as are the ankles. To assess for external rotation deformity, check the position of the patella and foot on each side. Roll the patient to one side to observe the buttock and posterior thigh for surgical scars and gluteal wasting. Ask your patient to stand towards the end of the examination when you are about to perform the Trendelenburg test and assess gait. It is always worth glancing at the hands for signs of osteoarthritis, and commenting on their presence or absence in your presentation.

Common OSCE cases

Arthritis of the hip

The patient may have an antalgic gait, contractures resulting in fixed adduction and flexion deformities, and the leg may be held in external rotation. There may be limited movement in the joint and apparent leg shortening due to pelvic tilt on the affected side. You may note signs of osteoarthritis in the hands, confirming your diagnosis.

Antalgic gait

This is due to a painful hip or knee. There is a shortened weight-bearing phase on the side affected by pain.

Trendelenburg gait

Due to inefficient hip abduction in the affected hip, the pelvis falls instead of rising on the opposite side whilst walking. A Trendelenburg gait is caused by weakness of the hip abductors (gluteus minimus and medius), which when unilateral is usually due to a neuropathy and when bilateral to a myopathy.

Key investigations

X-rays of the affected hip and corresponding knee
Bloods: full blood count (FBC), erythrocyte sedimentation rate (ESR), bone profile

KNEE JOINT

Mrs De Silva is a 67-year-old lady complaining of pain in her left knee. Please take a very short history of the pain, perform an appropriate examination and present your findings to the examiner.

Makes appropriate introduction of self and seeks permission to take a history and examine
Confirms patient's name and age

 ## History

Enquires about the site of the pain
Enquires about the degree of pain
Enquires about mobility, walking aids and lifestyle implications
Asks if the patient is currently in pain

 ## Look

Ensures patient is in supine position with both legs fully exposed
Inspects and compares both legs (looking for skin changes, swelling – especially in popliteal fossa, muscle wasting, varus/valgus deformities, surgical scars)

 ## Feel

Measures leg circumference (at fixed point above tibial tuberosity) to quantify muscle wasting
Assesses temperature of both legs
Assesses for a joint effusion (performs bulge or patellar tap test)
Palpates anterior and posterior joint line and comments on presence/absence of bony tenderness
Palpates popliteal fossa

 ## Move

Assesses flexion (active and passive)
Assesses extension (active and passive)
Assesses collateral ligaments (medial and lateral)
Assesses cruciate ligaments (anterior and posterior)
Assesses for torn meniscus – McMurray's test
Checks for distal neurovascular deficit (palpates left pedal pulses and briefly assesses for motor and sensory function of left foot)
Assesses gait

Cleans hands by washing or using alcohol gel

 ## Global marks

Fluency of examination
Competence in presenting findings, summarizing and forming differential diagnosis

KEY TIPS ⚬━●

Examination of the knee, like the hip, is quite physically challenging and requires practising in order to appear fluent. Attending orthopaedic or rheumatology outpatients will prove fruitful, as will practice on your friends.

Start the examination with your patient lying down. Whilst assessing passive movement, comment on the presence or absence of joint crepitus. Towards the end of your examination, ask the patient to stand in order for you to assess his/her gait and mobility; this also proves to be a good opportunity for inspecting the popliteal fossae. Concentrate on perfecting the basic aspects of your examination and do not worry too much about the specialist tests such as McMurray's test; as you can see from the mark-sheet opposite, they account for a small proportion of the overall marks.

Common OSCE cases

Osteoarthritis

The knee may be the only joint affected, and may be painful and stiff. On examination, there may be bony overgrowth, genu varum, a small joint effusion, joint crepitus, and limitation of joint movement. You should check the hands for Bouchard's and Heberden's nodes.

Rheumatoid arthritis

Knee involvement here is likely to be part of a generalized syndrome involving multiple joints. Pain and stiffness are also features. On examination, there may be a palpable synovium, genu valgum, a joint effusion, joint crepitus, limitation of movement and joint instability. Look at the hands for features of rheumatoid arthritis.

Knee deformities

Genu valgum or genu varum.

Key investigations

X-ray of the affected knee
Bloods: FBC, ESR, rheumatoid factor, bone profile

HANDS

Mrs Williams has a long-standing history of painful hands. Please take a very short history and examine her hands.

Introduces self and seeks permission to take a history and examine
Confirms patient's name and age

 ## History

Enquires about nature and degree of pain, stiffness and swelling
Establishes which joints are affected
Enquires about impact on lifestyle and functional abilities
Asks if patient is currently in pain

 ## Look

Inspects skin and nails (looks for clubbing, pitting, ridging, onycholysis and infarcts in the nails)
Inspects for bony deformities
Inspects for muscle wasting (thenar and hypothenar eminences)
Inspects the elbows for rheumatoid nodules

 ## Feel

Assesses temperature of forearms and hands
Palpates the finger and wrist joints for tenderness and swelling

 ## Move

Examines passive and active movements of all the hand joints and the wrist joint (assessing pain, range of movement and the presence of crepitus)
Assesses functional abilities, for example ability to hold a cup, undo a button
Performs an assessment of power and sensation

Acknowledges patient's feelings and disability
Cleans hands by washing or using alcohol gel

Global marks

Fluency of examination
Competence in presenting findings, summarizing and forming differential diagnoses

KEY TIPS 🔑

During the examination, expose the arm to above the elbow and, if available, place a pillow on the patient's lap or desk to make the examination more comfortable. You should comment on anything obvious at the start of your examination, for example if you have been presented with a case of rheumatoid arthritis you could say 'There is a an obvious bilateral, symmetrical deforming arthropathy'. Look carefully for signs of psoriasis, in case you have been presented with a case of psoriatic arthropathy. To assess the neurology you need only check for light touch in the distribution of the median, ulnar and radial nerves; and assess grip and opposition strength and the power of thumb abduction and finger adduction. If, however, you suspect carpal tunnel syndrome, you will additionally need to perform Tinnels and Phalens tests.

Common OSCE cases

Rheumatoid arthritis

It is usually symmetrical and systemic. There may be bony deformities, for example ulnar deviation, Boutonniere's deformity, swan-neck deformities, subluxation of the metacarpophalangeal (MCP) joint, and z-thumb deformity. There may also be wasting of the small muscles of the hand, synovial thickening at the proximal interphalangeal and MCP joints and rheumatoid nodules at the elbows.

Osteoarthritis

Signs here may include Heberden's and Bouchard's nodes, squaring of the thumb, and bony swelling of the distal interphalangeal (DIP) joints.

Carpal tunnel syndrome

Features here may include sensory loss in the distribution of the ulnar nerve, and motor loss and wasting of the lumbricals, opponens pollicis, abductor pollicis brevis and flexor pollicis longus (LOAF). Tinnels and Phalens tests may be positive.

Psoriatic arthritis

This is an asymmetrical polyarthritis and may be very severe; it is often referred to as 'arthritis mutilans'. There will also be other signs of psoriasis, for example the classical psoriatic rash, nail pitting and ridging and onycholysis. Its appearance may be similar to that of rheumatoid arthritis.

Key investigations

X-rays
Bloods: FBC, ESR, rheumatoid factor as appropriate

BACK

You are a PRHO in general practice. Mr Chan, a 30-year-old gentleman, presents to the practice complaining of sudden onset lower back pain radiating into his right leg. Please take a brief history and examine his back.

Introduces self and seeks permission to take a history and examine
Confirms patient's name and age

 ## History

Asks about onset of pain
Establishes site, nature and severity of pain
Enquires about neurological symptoms – numbness, tingling, weakness and bladder and bowel symptoms
Enquires about mobility
Briefly establishes past medical history and general health status
Asks if patient is currently in any pain

 ## Examination

Stands patient up fully exposed wearing only undergarments
Inspects for surgical scars, pigmentation, abnormal hair, scoliosis, kyphosis, loss of lumbar lordosis
Asks patient to pinpoint site of pain
Palpates vertebral bodies for tenderness and para-vertebral muscles for spasm
Assesses movements of neck, thoracic and lumbar spines
Assesses gait
Assesses for sacroiliac joint tenderness and performs femoral stretch test with patient prone
Performs straight-leg raising test with patient lying supine
Assesses hip abduction/adduction and internal/external rotation passively
Assesses neurological status of lower limbs appropriately
Assesses pedal pulses, moving proximally if not present
States intention to assess peri-anal sensation and anal tone

Cleans hands by washing or using alcohol gel

Global marks

Fluency of examination
Competence in presenting findings, summarizing and forming differential diagnoses

KEY TIPS 🔑

Assess the neck by asking your patient to perform forward flexion, extension and lateral flexion. Next assess the lumbar spine. To do this, ask your patient to touch his/her toes, lean back, and run a hand alongside the lateral aspect of each leg. Pain on flexion is suggestive of a prolapsed disc and one side should be affected more than the other, unless a very large disc has prolapsed. You will need to ask your patient to sit in order to assess the rotation movements of the thoracic spine, and, once sitting, to rotate his/her upper body to each side. Next ask your patient to lie prone, palpate the sacroiliac joint lines for tenderness and press on the midline of the sacrum to establish whether movement of the sacroiliac joints is painful. A painful femoral stretch test suggests irritation of nerve roots L2, L3 and L4, and a painful straight-leg raising test is suggestive of sciatica with nerve roots L5 and S1 being affected. Whilst performing these two tests you are also assessing hip flexion and extension, and the other hip movements should be assessed passively.

You do not need to perform a complete neurological assessment of the lower limb. You should assess for light touch in all the dermatomes, and test the knee and ankle reflexes. In terms of power, you will have already gauged power at the hip joint whilst assessing hip flexion and extension, so at this stage you need only assess the power of knee flexion/extension and ankle dorsiflexion and plantarflexion. You will need to be familiar with dermatomes and nerve root values.

Common OSCE cases

Muscular back pain

Disc prolapse

Pain is confined to the lower lumbar area and/or may radiate to the buttock or leg, exacerbated by coughing, sneezing and twisting. Forward flexion and extension are usually limited.

- L5–S1 prolapse causes compression of the S1 root, which may result in a diminished ankle jerk, weakness of plantarflexion and sensory loss along the lateral border of the foot and the sole.
- L4–L5 prolapse causes compression of the L5 root, which may result in weakness of foot dorsiflexion and sensory loss on the outer aspect of the leg and the dorsum of the foot.

Osteoarthritis

Ankylosing spondylitis

Key investigations

Plain X-rays, magnetic resonance imaging (MRI) as appropriate
Bloods: FBC, ESR, bone profile

RESPIRATORY SYSTEM

This is Mr Wong, a 62-year-old man complaining of shortness of breath and cough. Please examine his respiratory system.

Introduces self and seeks permission to examine
Confirms patient's name and age
Asks if patient is currently in any pain

Positions patient at 45° and fully exposes chest
Counts respiratory rate
Inspects hands for clubbing, nicotine staining and peripheral cyanosis
Checks for carbon dioxide retention flap and beta-agonist tremor
Examines head for clinical anaemia and central cyanosis
Examines neck for cervical lymphadenopathy and raised jugular venous pressure (JVP), and checks position of trachea
Inspects chest for chest movements, scars and deformity (anteriorly and posteriorly)
Palpates chest – assesses chest expansion and palpates for position of apex
Percusses chest
Assesses tactile vocal fremitus or vocal resonance
Auscultates chest
Examines for ankle oedema
Offers a measurement of peak flow

Cleans hands by washing or using alcohol gel

Global marks

Fluency of examination
Competence in presenting findings, summarizing and forming differential diagnoses

KEY TIPS ━●

Whilst measuring the respiratory rate you should also observe the patient for chest wall deformity, the use of accessory muscles of respiration, symmetrical chest wall movements, and pursed lip breathing. When inspecting for scars, have a good look front and back for signs of lobectomy, thoracotomy and drain sites.

The easiest way to examine the actual thorax is to start anteriorly and assess palpation, percussion, tactile vocal fremitus or vocal resonance and auscultation before repeating it all posteriorly. Remember to begin all these tests at the apices and move from side to side symmetrically down to the bases, not forgetting the axillae and lateral chest walls. Your examination technique is important and you should ensure that whilst assessing for chest wall expansion your thumbs are in the air at right-angles to the chest wall and not touching the patient's chest. Whilst percussing the chest, demonstrate a good tapping technique, and whilst assessing for tactile vocal fremitus, use the ulnar border of both hands simultaneously, one on each half of the chest wall. At the end of your examination, say that you would like to check the observation chart, do a peak flow measurement and, if appropriate, look in the sputum pot.

Common OSCE cases

Cryptogenic fibrosing alveolitis

Fine inspiratory basal crepitations, 60 per cent have finger clubbing, may be using oxygen, and may have steroidal skin/cushinoid features. (NB. Sarcoidosis and asbestosis can also cause lower lobe lung fibrosis resulting in lower lobe crepitations, and these and right heart failure will be your differential diagnoses.)

Chronic obstructive pulmonary disease

Signs of emphysema are hyperinflated and hyper-resonant lungs and quiet heart sounds and a non-palpable apex beat. Bronchitis results in widespread expiratory wheeze, and there may be basal crackles secondary to cor pulmonale.

Old tuberculosis

The patient is likely to be elderly. The trachea may be displaced to the side of the collapse and there may be apical signs of crackles, reduced expansion, dull percussion note, decreased tactile vocal fremitus and bronchial breathing.

Pleural effusion

Reduced chest expansion on the affected side, decreased tactile vocal fremitus, stony dull percussion note, reduced breath sounds. May be an exudate or a transudate – know the causes and look for surgical scars and radiotherapy marks suggestive of cancer.

Key investigations

Chest X-ray
Bloods: FBC, C-reactive protein (CRP)

GASTROINTESTINAL SYSTEM

Mr Desai is a 60-year-old gentleman complaining of abdominal pain. Please examine his gastrointestinal system.

Introduces self and seeks permission to examine
Confirms patient's name and age
Asks if patient is currently in any pain

Positions patient supine with one pillow, with abdomen exposed to groin
Inspects hands for clubbing, leuconychia, liver asterixis, palmar erythema and Dupuytren's contracture
Inspects eyes for jaundice and clinical anaemia
Palpates for cervical lymphadenopathy (Virchow's node)
Inspects trunk back and front for spider naevi and gynaecomastia
Inspects abdomen for scars, distension, masses, dilated abdominal veins and ascites
Palpates the abdomen, superficial and deep in all four quadrants whilst observing the face for tenderness
Palpates and percusses for hepatomegaly starting in the right iliac fossa
Palpates and percusses for splenomegaly starting in the right iliac fossa
Ballots kidneys
Palpates and percusses for a distended bladder
Palpates the abdominal aorta
Auscultates for bowel sounds and abdominal aorta bruit
Inspects and examines the groin for hernias
Offers to perform a digital rectal examination and examination of genitalia
If appropriate, offers to examine for shifting dullness

Cleans hands by washing or using alcohol gel

Global marks

Fluency of examination
Competence in presenting findings, summarizing and forming differential diagnoses

KEY TIPS →●

State to the examiner that you would normally expose the patient from nipple to groin but for the purposes of this particular examination you will expose the abdomen only. Obviously, when you come to examine the groin you will need to expose it for a short time. Stand at the end of the bed and observe for jaundice, abdominal distension and wasting. Whilst looking for scars, remember to look in the loins or you may miss a nephrectomy scar. To palpate the abdomen you need to get onto your knees, or raise the level of the bed, ensuring that your forearm and hand are flat against the patient's abdomen.

Do not forget to state at the end of your examination that you would like to examine the rectum and genitalia, and look at the observation chart and dipstix test the urine.

Common OSCE cases

Hepatomegaly

Comment on whether the liver edge is smooth, nodular or pulsatile and on whether there is decompensation of liver function – i.e. systemic signs of liver failure.
(Causes: alcoholic liver disease, congestive cardiac failure, carcinomatosis, hepatitis.)

Splenomegaly

Bruising and purpura may be a clue.
(Causes: chronic myeloid leukaemia, myelofibrosis, chronic lymphatic leukaemia and glandular fever.)

Hepatosplenomegaly

(Causes: myeloproliferative disease, lymphoproliferative disease, but most commonly cirrhosis with portal hypertension.)

Renal masses

The presence of an A-V fistula should be a clue.
(Causes: unilateral enlargement is due to a renal cyst, hydronephrosis, a renal neoplasm, and polycystic kidneys. Bilateral enlargement is due to polycystic kidneys and bilateral hydronephrosis. You may also be presented with a transplanted kidney.)

Hernias

(Inguinal, femoral, peri-umbilical, incisional and ventral.)

Abdominal aortic aneurysm

There will be expansile pulsatility.

Key investigations

Ultrasound scan
Bloods: FBC, renal function, liver function tests (LFTs), clotting screen

CARDIOVASCULAR SYSTEM

Mr Stoker is a 55-year-old gentleman who has presented to the accident and emergency department complaining of chest pain. Please examine his cardiovascular system.

Introduces self and seeks permission to examine
Confirms patient's name and age
Asks patient if he is currently in any pain

Positions patient at 45° with chest exposed
Examines hands for clubbing, signs of infective endocarditis, pallor, peripheral cyanosis and capillary refill
Assesses radial and carotid pulses (rate, rhythm, character)
Offers a blood pressure measurement
Inspects head for signs of clinical anaemia, cyanosis, xanthelasma, corneal arcus and malar flush
Inspects for a raised JVP
Inspects chest for scars and visible apex beat
Palpates chest for nature and site of the apex beat, and for any heaves or thrills
Auscultates praecordium in all four areas with patient appropriately positioned
Auscultates in the left axilla for radiation, and the carotids for radiation/bruits
Auscultates the lung bases
Palpates the peripheral pulses
Feels for sacral and ankle oedema

Cleans hands by washing or using alcohol gel

Global marks

Fluency of examination
Competence in presenting findings, summarizing and forming differential diagnoses

KEY TIPS ⚷

Whilst assessing the radial pulse, palpate both at the same time and comment on whether there is any radio-radial delay. Also check to see whether the pulse is slow rising or collapsing and if it is regular. It is worth inspecting carefully for scars, as these will give you clues to the diagnosis: a median sternotomy scar with vein harvest scars on the legs is suggestive of a coronary artery bypass graft; a median sternotomy scar alone and a lateral thoracotomy scar are suggestive of valvular replacement.

Make sure that you are fluent and well-practised in auscultating the heart in all four areas. Know how the patient should be positioned for each area and whether he/she should be holding his/her breath. If you tell the patient that you are checking his/her lower back and ankles for fluid, you will alert the examiner to the fact that you have carried out this step.

If you have heard a murmur, describe whether it is systolic or diastolic, where it is loudest, where it radiates to and what other abnormal findings there are on the cardiovascular examination. If possible, say what you think the most likely diagnosis is whilst giving other differential diagnoses. It is often difficult to identify exactly what murmur you have heard by clinical examination alone, and it is perfectly reasonable to state simply whether it is systolic or diastolic and that you would confirm the diagnosis with an echocardiogram.

At the end of the examination state that you would like to look at the observation chart, and in suspected cases of bacterial endocarditis dipstix test the urine. There is an excellent CD of murmurs which comes with some stethoscopes, and a good way to practise identifying different murmurs is to play it on random and test yourself. Pre-operative patients on cardiothoracic wards are also useful for practising listening to murmurs.

Common OSCE cases

Systolic murmur

(Most common cases are aortic stenosis and mitral regurgitation.)
Differential diagnoses for a systolic murmur are aortic stenosis, mitral regurgitation, aortic sclerosis, ventricular septal defect, pulmonary stenosis and tricuspid regurgitation.

Diastolic murmur

Differential diagnoses for a diastolic murmur are aortic regurgitation, mitral stenosis, tricuspid stenosis, pulmonary regurgitation.

Valve replacements

There will be either a median sternotomy or a lateral thoracotomy scar. A replaced mitral valve produces a loud click at the first heart sound, and a replaced aortic valve at the second. Always comment on whether the valve is functioning well or whether valve replacement surgery has been complicated by leakage or endocarditis.

Key investigations

Electrocardiogram (ECG), echocardiogram, chest X-ray
Bloods: lipid profile and, if bacterial endocarditis is suspected, CRP, FBC and blood cultures

BREAST

You are a PRHO in general practice. Mrs Nkwo is a middle-aged lady who has presented complaining of mastalgia of her right breast. Please take a relevant history and examine this lady's breasts.

Introduces self and seeks permission to take a history and examine
Confirms patient's name and age

 ## History

Establishes rapport and addresses patient's concerns
Establishes history of the presenting complaint
Enquires about nipple discharge (asks specifically whether unilateral or bilateral, what colour, and if appropriate whether she has been breast-feeding recently)
Enquires about past medical history of breast diseases
Enquires about menarche and menopause
Enquires about hormone replacement therapy and the oral contraceptive pill, and takes a general drug history
Enquires about any family history of breast disease
Enquires about previous breast investigations the patient may have had
Asks if patient is currently in any pain

 ## Examination

Positions patient lying at 45° with chest exposed
Inspects for: size, symmetry, presence of nipple retraction or distortion, eczema, peau d'orange, skin dimpling, skin tethering, nipple discharge
Palpates breasts in all four quadrants
Examines axillae
Percusses and auscultates lung bases
Palpates vertebrae for bony tenderness
Examines for hepatomegaly
Examines for cervical and supraclavicular lymphadenopathy

Cleans hands by washing or using alcohol gel

 ## Global marks

Fluency of examination
Competence in presenting findings, summarizing and forming differential diagnoses

KEY TIPS ━●

In this station particularly, you need to be sensitive and careful to avoid discomfort and embarrassment. During the history taking, if your patient is presenting with a breast lump, you must establish how long the lump has been there, whether it has changed at all and whether it changes with the menstrual cycle.

Start the examination with the lady lying at 45° with her thorax exposed and arms placed by her sides. Inspection is commenced with the patient in this position, but to look for tethering you will need to ask her to place her hands behind her head, and then to press her hands against her hips. For palpation, her hands should remain behind her head.

Ask the patient to point with one finger to the lump if that is what she is presenting with, and start by palpating the normal breast. You should examine all four quadrants systematically, ending with the nipple, and then conduct a specific examination of any lump. You should also examine the lung bases, vertebrae and liver for distant metastases.

Maintain the patient's dignity at all times, by covering the breasts whilst examining other systems.

Common OSCE cases

Fibroadenoma

The patient is usually young, approximately 25 to 35 years of age. The lump is small and rubbery hard, and there may be more than one lump present. The lumps are usually very mobile, and are known as 'breast mice' for that reason. They are usually pain free.

Fibroadenosis

This is a very common condition, affecting women of reproductive age. It presents with single/multiple lumps, and these may be solid or cystic. On palpation, there is a diffuse lumpy feeling, often in the upper outer quadrant. Other features are cyclical mastalgia, and sometimes there is a nipple discharge, which may be clear, white or green.

Breast cyst

Key investigations

Mammogram and/or ultrasound scan of breast
Fine-needle aspiration or core biopsy

NECK

You are a PRHO in general practice; a 45-year-old lady has presented to you complaining of a neck swelling, which she has had for some time. Please take a short history from her and examine her neck.

Introduces self and seeks permission to take a history and examine
Confirms patient's name and age

 ## History

Establishes how long the swelling has been present and whether it has changed over time
Enquires about any local effects of the swelling, in particular pain, difficulty swallowing and difficulty breathing
Asks if patient is currently in any pain

 ## Examination

Ensures patient is sitting upright in a chair with the neck exposed
Inspects neck from the front and side – commenting on the presence/absence of surgical scars, asymmetry, and any obvious swellings
Inspects for movement of swelling whilst patient takes a sip of water, and protrudes tongue
Palpates swelling
Palpates for movement of swelling whilst patient takes a sip of water, and protrudes tongue
Palpates for cervical lymphadenopathy
Assesses for tracheal deviation
Auscultates over swelling for thyroid bruit

Cleans hands by washing or using alcohol gel

 ## Global marks

Fluency of examination
Competence in presenting findings, summarizing and forming differential diagnoses

KEY TIPS 🔑

Read the instructions to this station carefully. If you have been asked to examine the neck, the mark-sheet opposite is adequate; however, if you have been asked to examine the thyroid gland, there are some additional things you will need to do and these are described in the following station.

Any swelling should be described in terms of whether it is a midline swelling or in the right/left anterior/posterior triangle. During palpation, comment on the features of the swelling – unilateral/bilateral, tender, diffusely enlarged, solitary nodule, multi-nodular, size, texture and surface.

Common OSCE cases

Thyroid enlargement with normal function
Thyroid neoplasm (adenoma, carcinoma, lymphoma)
Thyroglossal cyst
Enlarged lymph nodes

Key investigations

Ultrasound scan blood tests as appropriate

THYROID

You are a PRHO in general practice; a 25-year-old woman has presented to you complaining of a neck swelling and weight loss. Please take a short history from her and examine her thyroid gland.

Introduces self and seeks permission to take a history and examine
Confirms patient's name and age

History

Establishes how long the swelling has been present and whether it has changed over time
Enquires about any local effects of the swelling, in particular pain, difficulty swallowing and difficulty breathing
Enquires about systemic effects of thyroid disease – change in weight, extreme preference for hot/cold temperatures, change in bowel habit, lethargy and change in mood
Asks if patient is currently in any pain

Examination

Inspects from the end of the bed for signs of thyroid disease
Inspects neck from the front and side, commenting on the presence/absence of surgical scars, asymmetry and any obvious swellings
Inspects for movement of swelling whilst patient takes a sip of water
Palpates swelling
Palpates for movement of swelling whilst patient takes a sip of water
Palpates for cervical lymphadenopathy
Assesses for tracheal deviation
Auscultates over swelling for thyroid bruit
Measures radial pulse rate
Examines hands for sweatiness, palmar erythema, thyroid acropachy and a postural tremor
Examines eyes for lid lag and ophthalmoplegia
Assesses for proximal myopathy

Cleans hands by washing or using alcohol gel

Global marks

Fluency of examination
Competence in presenting findings, summarizing and forming differential diagnoses

KEY TIPS 🔑

Start the examination with a general inspection for signs of thyroid disease. Look at the face for the presence of peri-orbital puffiness and loss of the outer third of the eyebrows, and observe whether the skin is dry or shiny and the hair coarse/dry/thinning. Note your patient's build and also whether he/she is dressed appropriately for the temperature. The presence of any of these signs will be clues to the differential diagnosis, and if they fit the rest of your examination, should be included in your presentation.

Common OSCE cases

Thyroid enlargement with normal function

Toxic goitre

Diffuse (Graves' disease)
Multinodular
Toxic nodule (Plummer's disease)

Hashimoto's thyroiditis
Thyroid neoplasm

Key investigations

Ultrasound scan
Thyroid function tests

GROIN

Mr Croker is a 57-year-old builder who has noticed a new swelling in his groin. Please take a brief history and examine his inguinoscrotal region.

Introduces self and seeks permission to take a history and examine
Confirms patient's name and age

History

Establishes onset and duration of swelling, and how it troubles the patient (e.g. pain, tenderness)
Asks if patient is currently in any pain

Examination

Stands patient up and exposes groin/scrotum adequately
Inspects scrotum
Palpates testes, epididymydes and spermatic cords
Defines characteristics of scrotal swelling if present (size, shape, fluctuant, transilluminable, cough impulse)
Assesses groin swelling if present (size, shape, fluctuant, transilluminable, cough impulse)
Demonstrates inguinal ligament (in relation to pubic tubercle and ASIS)
Examines superficial inguinal rings for a cough impulse
Lies patient down
If inguinal hernia suspected, assesses whether direct or indirect
Palpates femoral arteries, assessing for an aneurysm
Examines for lymphadenopathy

Ensures patient is re-clothed and washes hands

Global marks

Fluency of examination
Competence in presenting findings, summarizing and forming differential diagnoses

KEY TIPS ━●

Important anatomical landmarks are:

mid-inguinal point – halfway between the ASIS and pubic symphysis at the location of the femoral pulse,

mid-point of the inguinal ligament – halfway between the ASIS and the pubic tubercle, and this is the location of the deep inguinal ring,

superficial inguinal ring – this is located above and medial to the pubic tubercle.

Start the examination with your patient standing up exposing the groin and scrotum. If on general inspection there is an obvious swelling, describe it to the examiner. To examine the scrotum, first observe the anterior aspect for skin changes and the presence of a scrotal swelling. Then observe the posterior aspect before moving on to palpation. If there is a scrotal swelling, define its characteristics and determine whether you can get above the swelling, i.e. is it an indirect inguinal hernia or a swelling originating in the scrotum? Ascertain also whether the swelling is separate from the testis – if so, it is likely to be an epididymal cyst or a spermatocele; if not, it is likely to be a testicular tumour or a hydrocele. There is a simple way to determine whether an inguinal hernia is direct or indirect – ask the patient to reduce the hernia when he is lying down and place your two fingers over the deep inguinal ring, then ask him to cough. An indirect inguinal hernia will be controlled by pressure over the deep inguinal ring, and a direct inguinal hernia will not.

Common OSCE cases

Hydrocele

Femoral hernia

Below the inguinal ligament, inferior and lateral to the pubic tubercle.

Indirect inguinal hernia

Superior and medial to the pubic tubercle, extending into the scrotum and controlled by pressure over the deep inguinal ring.

Direct inguinal hernia

Superior and medial to the pubic tubercle, and not controlled by pressure over the deep inguinal ring.

Saphena varix

This is a varicosity in the saphenous vein at its confluence with the femoral vein. It normally has a cough impulse and a bluish tinge and disappears on lying down.

Femoral artery aneurysm

An expansile, pulsatile mass. A bruit may be present.

Key investigations

Ultrasound scan

LYMPHADENOPATHY

This 49-year-old gentleman is presenting with a mass in his right axilla. Please take a short history and conduct an appropriate examination of the mass and relevant systems.

Introduces self and seeks permission to take a history and examine
Confirms patient's name and age

History

Enquires about onset and duration of the mass
Enquires about changes to the mass over time
Enquires about how the mass troubles the patient (pain, tenderness)
Asks if patient is currently in any pain

Examination

Exposes and positions patient appropriately
Inspects for any obvious lymphadenopathy
Examines hands for clubbing and arms for any lesions which may give rise to axillary lymphadenopathy
Inspects conjunctivae for signs of clinical anaemia
Inspects tonsils
Examines cervical lymph nodes
Examines supraclavicular lymph nodes
Examines axillary lymph nodes, including specific examination of the mass
If cervical/supraclavicular/axillary lymphadenopathy is present, appropriately examines above the umbilicus for any skin, lung, breast, intra-abdominal, ear, mouth or throat lesions which could be the cause
Examines for hepatomegaly and splenomegaly
Examines inguinal nodes
If inguinal lymphadenopathy is present, examines inguinal lymph node drainage areas for possible cause

Cleans hands by washing or using alcohol gel

Global marks

Fluency of examination
Competence in presenting findings, summarizing and forming differential diagnoses

KEY TIPS 🔑

The instructions opposite clearly inform you that a full systems examination is required; however, you may not benefit from such clear instructions in your final OSCE. Remember that in addition to an examination of the enlarged node you should also conduct a full examination of the lymphatic system.

Your patient should be undressed to his/her undergarments and lying at 45°, initially with the groin and legs covered with a sheet. To examine the cervical nodes, stand behind the patient and use the fingers of both hands, assessing each side simultaneously. Begin with the submental node, moving to the submandibular nodes, jugular chain, posterior triangle nodes, occipital region, post-auricular nodes and finally pre-auricular nodes. There are five groups of axillary nodes: apical/central, lateral, medial/pectoral, anterior and posterior. The inguinal lymph nodes are divided into a horizontal and a vertical chain; the horizontal chain is just below the inguinal ligament and the vertical chain lies along the saphenous vein. Whilst examining the inguinal nodes you can ask your patient to wear his/her upper clothing to help maintain dignity.

To assess an enlarged lymph node you need to describe its site, size, consistency, whether it is tender, whether there is fixation to underlying surfaces and if there is tethering/inflammation of the overlying skin. A lymph node greater than 1 cm in size is abnormal. A stony-hard consistency and fixation and tethering of the overlying skin are suggestive of malignancy. A rubbery-hard node suggests lymphoma. Since the cervical lymph nodes drain the head and neck, if lymphadenopathy is present, you should examine the mouth and throat with a pen torch and the ears with an otoscope, and inspect the face and scalp carefully for any skin lesions. The horizontal group of inguinal nodes drains the abdomen below the umbilicus, the buttock and back, and the skin of the penis, scrotum, perineum, lower vagina, vulva and anus. The vertical group drains the lower limb.

Common OSCE cases

Localized lymphadenopathy

Neoplastic metastases
Lymphoma

Generalized lymphadenopathy

Infective/reactive (e.g. human immunodeficiency virus infection)
Infiltrative: metastatic disease, lymphoma
Others: sarcoidosis, connective tissue disease, dermatopathic, e.g. eczema

Key investigations

Radiology: ultrasound scan of the mass, and imaging of suspected causative pathology
Bloods: FBC and differential, renal function, LFTs, bone profile, CRP, ESR monospot test, and blood film if indicated

VENOUS

Mrs Huntley is a 40 year-old lady who is complaining of painful varicose veins. Please take a short history and examine her legs with respect to the venous system.

Introduces self and seeks permission to take a history and examine
Confirms patient's name and age

 ## History

Asks patient about site and degree of pain
Asks if patient is currently in any pain

 ## Examination

Adequately exposes both legs with the patient standing up
Inspects both legs (compares for shape; and comments on the presence/absence of previous surgery, skin changes above the medial malleolus and distribution of varicosities, including a saphena varix in the groin)
Assesses the temperature of both legs
Assesses for tenderness and palpates along the medial side of the lower leg
Palpates the sapheno-femoral junction for a cough impulse (suggestive of sapheno-femoral incompetence)
Palpates the sapheno-popliteal junction for a cough impulse (suggestive of sapheno-popliteal incompetence)
If a saphena varix is present, palpates it for a cough impulse
Performs the tap test (a percussion impulse is suggestive of incompetence in the superficial veins)
Performs the Trendelenburg test (if the veins are controlled by a tourniquet or fingers at the sapheno-femoral junction, this is suggestive of sapheno-femoral incompetence)
If the Trendelenburg test is negative, performs the tourniquet test to find the level at which venous incompetence lies
Auscultates for a bruit over marked venous clusters
Examines the peripheral pulses (femoral, popliteal, dorsalis pedis and posterior tibial)

Cleans hands by washing or using alcohol gel

Global marks

Fluency of examination
Competence in presenting findings, summarizing and forming differential diagnoses

KEY TIPS

In this station you will need to have a good knowledge of basic lower limb venous anatomy. It is one of the harder examination stations and time is usually tight; it is well worth attending a session or two in a vascular outpatient clinic followed by lots of practice on unsuspecting friends and family!

Ask your patient to stand up once you are ready to start examining. Whilst inspecting, look at the anterior and posterior aspects of the legs, and run the back of your hand down both legs to assess for temperature. The tap test should only be performed if there are long visible varicosities, and it should be performed with the patient standing up. You should then ask the patient to lie down in order for you to perform the Trendelenburg and tourniquet tests.

Whilst presenting your findings, say that you would like to perform a digital rectal examination, examine the abdomen, and examine the external genitalia in males and pelvis in females. This is to exclude an abdominal or pelvic mass that may be causing inferior vena cava obstruction.

Common OSCE cases

Varicose veins

By definition, the presence of dilated, tortuous superficial veins.

Venous insufficiency

There may be skin changes such as eczema, venous ulcers and pigmentation due to haemosiderin deposition. It is divided into superficial and deep venous insufficiency, the superficial form involving mild skin changes due to incompetent *perforator* veins (hence resulting in blood flow from the deep to the superficial system). In deep venous insufficiency there are more severe skin changes, and there may be other features such as champagne bottle leg (due to oedema and dermatoliposclerosis). It is due to incompetent *deep* veins resulting in raised pressure in the deep system.

Key investigations

Doppler ultrasound scan

ARTERIAL

Mr Tang is a 58-year-old man complaining of pain on walking. Please examine his peripheral vascular system, concentrating on his legs.

Introduces self and seeks permission to examine
Confirms patient's name and age

Exposes legs adequately
Asks whether patient is in pain
Inspects for ischaemic skin changes, ulcers and surgical scars (looks especially for ulcers on the tips of the toes and around the heels)
Assesses the temperature of both legs
Checks for capillary refilling time
Feels for pulses: abdominal aorta, femoral, popliteal, posterior tibial and dorsalis pedis
Auscultates for bruits (femoral and popliteal)
Assesses for venous guttering (elevates the leg to approximately 15°)
Checks Buerger's angle (this is the angle at which the leg becomes pale)
Performs Buerger's test (after checking Buerger's angle, asks the patient to hang his legs over the side of the bed – looks for reactive hyperaemia)
States intention to examine the rest of the peripheral vascular system
States intention to examine the cardiovascular system
States intention to perform an ankle–brachial pressure index (ABPI) reading using a hand-held Doppler

Cleans hands by washing or using alcohol gel

Global marks

Fluency of examination
Competence in presenting findings, summarizing and forming differential diagnoses

KEY TIPS ⚬

Read the instructions to this station carefully – you may only be required to examine the legs and merely mention your intent to examine the rest, or you may have to examine the whole peripheral vascular system. If the latter is the case, palpate both radial pulses checking for radio-radial delay, check for radio-femoral delay, listen for carotid artery bruits, inspect and palpate the abdominal aorta, and finally auscultate for common iliac bruits before moving on to the leg vasculature.

Whilst inspecting, comment on the colour of both legs and the presence/absence of trophic changes such as shiny skin, loss of hair and ulcers. Look also for the signs of gangrene – nail infections and amputation. Arterial ulcers are found particularly on the heel, on the lateral side of the foot, and on the tips of the toes. If an ulcer is present, describe it and consider whether it is arterial or secondary to other pathology.

Common OSCE cases

Intermittent claudication

The presentation may include the six Ps: pain, paraesthesia, pallor, pulselessness, paralysis, and perishing cold. You will need to distinguish between aorto-iliac disease where all the leg pulses are absent, and femoro-distal disease where only the popliteal and foot pulses are absent.

Critical ischaemia

This may present with trophic changes (hair loss, shiny skin, loss of subcutaneous tissue and ischaemic ulcers at pressure points), gangrene and a positive Buerger's test.

Diabetic foot

This may be red and warm with gangrene and infection. The pulses may be present. Briefly assess sensation to check for signs of peripheral neuropathy (this will help confirm your diagnosis).

Amputation

Assess for any social implications, ascertain whether it is a below-knee, through-knee or above-knee amputation, and check the wound site.

Key investigations

ABPI measurement, ECG, arteriogram
Blood lipid profile, and ulcer swab for infection

UPPER LIMB NEUROLOGY

Miss Levene has been complaining of weakness in her right arm. Please examine her upper limb neurology.

Introduces self and seeks permission to examine
Confirms patient's name and age
Asks about function
Asks if patient is currently in any pain

Positions patient appropriately, exposing both arms to the shoulder
Inspects arms and hands – looking for wasting and fasciculation
Assesses arms for tone
Tests power of shoulder abduction
Tests power of elbow flexion
Tests power of elbow extension
Tests power of wrist long flexors and extensors
Tests power of finger extension, abduction and adduction
Tests power of thumb abduction and opposition
Assesses reflexes (biceps, triceps and supinator) with reinforcement if necessary
Tests light touch and pinprick sensation in all dermatomes
Tests vibration sense and proprioception
Tests finger – nose coordination

Cleans hands by washing or using alcohol gel

Global marks

Fluency of examination
Competence in presenting findings, summarizing and forming differential diagnoses

KEY TIPS ━●

Each step of the examination as described in the scheme opposite should first be performed on one arm and then on the other, so you are always comparing both limbs. It is useful to prepare in advance clear instructions for your patient that allow easy understanding of what you want him/her to do.

You will need to know nerve root values and dermatomes in order to perform a succinct examination, interpret your findings and form differential diagnoses. Important nerve root values are listed below.

Shoulder abduction: C5
Elbow flexion: C6
Elbow extension: C7
Wrist flexion: C7, C8
Wrist extension: C6, C7
Finger extension: C7 (radial nerve)
Finger spread and adduction: T1 (ulnar nerve)
Thumb abduction and opposition: T1 (median nerve)
Biceps reflex: C5
Supinator reflex: C6
Triceps reflex: C7

To assess vibration sense, you should demonstrate it first in a normal area of sensation, then start testing at a distal phalanx, moving to a more proximal bony point, for example the wrist, elbow, shoulder or sternum, if found to be absent. Proprioception similarly should be assessed distally first, moving proximally if found to be absent.

Determining whether any motor deficit is due to an upper motor neurone (UMN) or lower motor neurone (LMN) lesion or a myopathy is necessary in order to form a differential diagnosis.

Common OSCE cases

Hemiparesis

Upper motor neurone signs, usually secondary to a cerebrovascular event.

Spastic quadriparesis/weakness

This is a UMN lesion caused by spinal cord compression, multiple sclerosis, and motor neurone disease (fasciculations are your clue, as there is also LMN involvement)

Ulnar/medial/radial nerve palsies

Carpal tunnel syndrome

Peripheral neuropathy

Myopathy

Due to polymyositis/dermatomyositis or a muscular dystrophy (Duchenne or myotonic).

Key investigations

Computerized tomography (CT) head, MRI, nerve conduction studies and electromyography as appropriate

LOWER LIMB NEUROLOGY

Please examine this gentleman's lower limb neurological system.

Introduces self and seeks permission to examine
Confirms patient's name and age
Asks if patient is currently in any pain

Positions patient appropriately, exposing both legs
Inspects lower limbs – looking for wasting and fasciculation
Assesses legs for tone, including testing for ankle clonus if tone is increased
Tests power of hip flexion
Tests power of hip extension
Tests power of knee flexion
Tests power of knee extension
Tests power of ankle dorsiflexion
Tests power of plantar flexion
Tests power of eversion of forefoot
Tests power of inversion of forefoot
Assesses reflexes (knee, ankle and plantar) with reinforcement if necessary
Tests light touch and pinprick sensation in all dermatomes
Tests vibration sense and proprioception
Tests heel–shin coordination
Observes gait– comments on posture, arm swing, step size and equality, ataxia and circumduction
Performs Romberg's test

Cleans hands by washing or using alcohol gel

Global marks

Fluency of examination
Competence in presenting findings, summarizing and forming differential diagnoses

KEY TIPS ⚫━

Start the examination with your patient lying in a semi-prone position with the legs fully exposed, asking him/her to stand at the end to assess gait and perform Romberg's test.

As for the upper limb neurology station, you will need to know nerve root values and dermatomes. Important nerve root values are listed below.

Hip flexion: L1, L2
Hip extension: S1
Knee flexion: L5, S1
Knee extension: L3, L4
Ankle dorsiflexion: L4, L5
Ankle plantar flexion: S1
Knee jerk: L3, L4
Ankle jerk: S1

As for the upper limb neurological examination, first demonstrate vibration sense to the patient in a normal area of sensation and then start testing distally at the greater toe, moving to more proximal bony points (medial malleolus, knee, iliac crest, sternum) if sensation is absent. Coordination is difficult to interpret in the presence of spasticity and weakness.

Common OSCE cases

Foot drop

L5 lesion (common peroneal nerve).

Hemiparesis

Upper motor neurone signs, usually secondary to a cerebrovascular event.

Spastic paraparesis

This is a UMN lesion caused by spinal cord compression, multiple sclerosis, and motor neurone disease (fasciculations are your clue, as there is also LMN involvement).

Peripheral neuropathy

Features are: distal muscle wasting/foot drop, Charcot joints, pes cavus, claw toes, distal weakness, absent ankle jerks, sensory involvement in both the dorsal columns and spinothalamic tracts, and possibly a sensory ataxic gait and positive Romberg's test.

Myopathy

Due to polymyositis/dermatomyositis or a muscular dystrophy (Duchenne or myotonic). There may be a waddling gait due to proximal muscle weakness.

Key investigations

CT head, MRI, nerve conduction studies, electromyography as appropriate

CRANIAL NERVES

Please examine Mrs Mensah's cranial nerves.

Introduces self and seeks permission to examine
Confirms patient's name and age
Asks if patient is currently in any pain

Conducts a general inspection (looking for ptosis, facial asymmetry)

   I: enquires about a change in sense of smell (offers formal olfactory examination if
      there hasbeen a change)
   II: offers examination of cranial nerve II
   III, IV, VI: assesses eye movements (enquires about diplopia and observes for
      nystagmus)
   V (sensation): assesses for light touch in the three trigeminal nerve areas, offers to
      assess pinprick sensation, and states intention to assess for a corneal reflex
   V (motor): assesses muscles of mastication (masseter and pterygoids) and offers to test
      for the jaw jerk reflex
   VII (sensation): states intention to assess the anterior two-thirds of the tongue for
      sensation
   VII (motor): tests for power in the upper and lower facial muscles
   VIII: assesses hearing of whispered sounds, and offers tuning fork tests and otoscopy
   IX: assesses palatal movements and offers to test for the gag reflex
   X: comments on phonation and offers to test for the gag reflex
   XI: assesses the power of sternocleidomastoid and trapezius muscles
   XII: examines the tongue for wasting, fasciculation and power

Cleans hands by washing or using alcohol gel

Global marks

Fluency of examination
Competence in presenting findings, summarizing and forming differential diagnoses

KEY TIPS ⚯

In a 7-minute cranial nerve examination station, you would not be able to perform a full examination of cranial nerves II and VIII. You may be asked to examine these in separate eye and hearing stations, and these have been included later in the chapter. You may not even be required to examine all ten of the other cranial nerves and the instructions will specify, for example you may be asked just to examine the lower cranial nerves (cranial nerves V to XII).

Common OSCE cases

Facial nerve palsy – lower and upper motor neurone

A LMN palsy is complete facial nerve palsy and its common causes are Bell's palsy, a demyelinating process and mononeuritis (diabetes mellitus). A UMN palsy is incomplete (the upper face is spared and the patient is able to raise his/her eyebrows) and its commonest cause is a cerebrovascular accident.

Cerebellopontine angle lesion

This affects cranial nerves V–VIII inclusive, and an acoustic neuroma should be considered.

Ptosis

The common causes of unilateral ptosis are Horner's syndrome and a lesion in cranial nerve III. Bilateral ptosis is commonly caused by myasthenia gravis or myotonic dystrophy.

Myasthenia gravis

Features are myotonic facies, fatiguable uni/bilateral ptosis, diplopia and fatiguable ophthalmoplegia, a weak voice and muscle weakness (proximal muscles are affected more than distal muscles).

Bulbar palsy (LMN)

Features are poor palatal movement and loss of gag reflex (cranial nerves IX and X); a weak, wasted and fasciculating tongue (cranial nerve XII – LMN); a poor cough impulse; and speech is of poor quality or nasal in nature. Causes are motor neurone disease, syringobulbia, Guillain–Barré and medullary pathology (vascular, demyelination or tumour).

Pseudobulbar palsy (UMN)

Features are poor palatal movement, a spastic tongue (cranial XII – UMN), a brisk jaw jerk and 'Donald Duck speech'. Causes are motor neurone disease and demyelination.

Multiple sclerosis

This could present with any central nervous system sign and it may be in isolation, for example ataxic nystagmus. Clues are a young and/or wheelchair bound patient.

Key investigations

CT/MRI scan of the head

CEREBELLAR FUNCTION

Mrs Barker, a 67-year-old lady, is complaining of being unsteady whilst walking. Please carry out a neurological examination to assess her balance and cerebellar function.

Introduces self and seeks permission to examine
Confirms patient's name and age
Enquires about relevant symptoms
Asks if patient is currently in any pain

Stands at the end of the bed and observes for presence of wheelchair, urinary catheter, titubation
Examines for nystagmus
Assesses for dysarthric speech (asks patient to say 'British constitution' or 'baby hippopotamus')
Assesses tone in upper limbs
Asks patient to perform finger–nose test, looking for upper limb ataxia
Assesses for dysdiadochokinesis (by observing rapid alternating hand movements)
Examines fine finger movements (asks patient to oppose each finger in turn against her thumb)
Assesses for cerebellar drift
Asks patient to perform heel–shin test, looking for lower limb ataxia
Assesses gait
Assesses tandem gait (asks patient to walk heel to toe)
Performs Romberg's test

Cleans hands by washing or using alcohol gel

Global marks

Fluency of examination
Competence in presenting findings, summarizing and forming differential diagnoses

KEY TIPS ⚯

An easy way to remember the features of cerebellar disease is to remember the following:

D: dysmetria (past pointing in finger–nose test and dysdiadochokinesis),
A: ataxia (finger–nose ataxia, heel–shin ataxia, ataxic gait – broad based and patient falls to side of lesion),
N: nystagmus (lesion is ipsilateral to the fast phase),
I: intention tremor elicited in finger–nose test,
S: slurring/staccato speech,
H: hypotonia, hyporeflexia.

To perform the finger–nose test, hold your index finger approximately 50 cm away from the patient's nose. Ask the patient to touch your finger with the index finger of his/her right hand, then to touch his/her nose, and then again to touch your finger. The patient should repeat this continuously as fast as possible. The test should then be repeated with the index finger of the patient's left hand. In cerebellar disease you will notice ataxia ipsilateral to the lesion, with past pointing and an intention tremor.

To perform the Romberg's test, ask the patient to stand upright with the feet slightly apart, initially with the eyes open and then with them closed. A marked sway with the eyes both open and closed is indicative of cerebellar disease; if the patient only sways with the eyes closed, dorsal column proprioceptive deficit should be suspected.

Common OSCE cases

Demyelination

Multiple sclerosis.

Cerebrovascular disease in posterior circulation

Haemorrhage or infarct.

Tumour in the posterior fossa
Degenerative

Alcohol related, Friedreich's ataxia.

Primary/idiopathic
Iatrogenic

Secondary to phenytoin or carbamazepine.

Key investigations

CT/MRI of the head

OPHTHALMOLOGY

Please examine Mrs Tyson's eyes.

Introduces self and seeks permission to examine
Confirms patient's name and age
Enquires about relevant symptoms – acuity, diplopia, visual field loss
Asks if patient is currently in any pain

Positions patient appropriately
Inspects for ptosis, squint, exophthalmos and pupil size and irregularity
Enquires about and tests for visual acuity (uses Snellen chart if one is available,
otherwise asks patient to read ordinary type face/count fingers; visual acuity should be
tested with spectacles or contact lenses if usually worn by the patient)
States intention to test colour vision using Ishihara colour plates
Assesses visual neglect (crude test for visual field loss)
Examines visual fields carefully (tests for a peripheral defect and uses red hat pin to
delineate the patient's blind spot and any scotomas, and to test for macular sparing)
Examines eye movements vertically and horizontally (enquires about diplopia and
observes for nystagmus)
Examines for pupillary light and accommodation reflexes
Sets and handles ophthalmoscope correctly
Assesses for a red reflex with the ophthalmoscope
Correct technique for viewing fundi
Correct technique for viewing discs

Cleans hands by washing or using alcohol gel

Global marks

Fluency of examination
Competence in presenting findings, summarizing and forming differential diagnoses

KEY TIPS ⚊●

Ophthalmologists use sophisticated equipment in clinic, negating the need for them to perform many of the steps opposite. For you to gain the most from an ophthalmology clinic, show the mark-sheet opposite and ask to be taught or observed according to the marking scheme, using basic equipment such as hat pins and a hand-held ophthalmoscope. There are also mannequins that you can practise on, and these are usually found in clinical skills centres.

Common OSCE cases (you may be shown a photograph of a retina)

Diabetic retinopathy/hypertensive retinopathy

This is probably the most common case, so be familiar with the appearances of hypertensive and diabetic retinopathy.

Homonymous hemianopia or a quadrantanopia

The usual pathology is cerebrovascular disease. A left homonymous hemianopia is due to pathology affecting the right optic radiation or visual cortex (posterior circulation infarct). A left superior quadrantanopia is caused by pathology in the right temporal lobe, and a left inferior quadrantanopia by pathology in the right parietal lobe.

Bitemporal hemianopia

This is usually due to a pituitary tumour compressing the optic chiasm, and if it grows more to one side than the other, it may result in a central optic nerve defect as well.

Optic atrophy

Other clinical signs may include decreased visual acuity, absence of afferent/direct pupillary light reflex (consensual reflex remains intact), a central scotoma, and a pale optic disc (with cupping of the rim if glaucoma is the cause). Other common causes are optic neuritis, demyelination and compression by a tumour.

Papilloedema

There will be an increase in the size of the blind spot and, on fundoscopy, blurred disc margins, swelling of the optic head, and hypertensive retinopathy if accelerated hypertension is the cause. The other common cause is an intracerebral space-occupying lesion.

Nystagmus (horizontal, vertical, ataxic)

An ipsilateral cerebellar/brainstem lesion or a contralateral vestibular lesion results in horizontal nystagmus. Vertical nystagmus on the up-gaze is caused by a lesion at the superior colliculus, and on the down-gaze by a lesion at the level of the foramen magnum. Ataxic nystagmus is due to multiple sclerosis and the patient may also demonstrate some other signs of the disease.

Monocular blindness

Causes of monocular blindness are macular degeneration, glaucoma and cataracts.

Ptosis

If bilateral, you should think of myasthenia gravis or myotonic dystrophy; if unilateral, think of Horner's or a third cranial nerve lesion.

NOSE

You are a PRHO in general practice and Miss Davies has come to see you complaining of a blocked nose. Please take a short history and conduct an examination of her nose.

Introduces self and seeks permission to take a history and examine
Confirms patient's name and age

History

Enquires about characteristics of nasal obstruction – unilateral/bilateral/alternating, is obstruction constant or does it vary with time of day/season?
Enquires about associated features – rhinorrhoea, facial pain, sneezing, swelling, itch, paroxysmal nocturnal dyspnoea, sense of smell, catarrh
Establishes impact on patient's life
Enquires about possible causes – allergies, hayfever, injury, pets, use of nasal sprays/drops
Enquires about previous ENT surgery
Asks if patient is currently in any pain

Examination

Positions patient appropriately
Examines the external nose (inspects for deformity and septal deviation)
Assesses nasal patency (using a metal tongue blade)
Assesses for functional/alar collapse
Examines internal nose with an otoscope (comments on septum, turbinate, mucosa and presence/absence of polyps)

Cleans hands by washing or using alcohol gel

Global marks

Fluency of examination
Competence in presenting findings, summarizing and forming differential diagnoses

KEY TIPS 🔑

As a medical student, examination of the nose is not something that you will have had much opportunity to practise and it is worth attending an ENT clinic to be taught how to do it properly and to familiarize yourself with the equipment that is required – tongue blade, special Thudicum speculum and an otoscope. To examine the nose, your patient should be positioned upright in a chair. To assess for septal deviation, you need to lift the tip of the patient's nose using your thumb. Nasal patency is assessed using a metal tongue blade; you block one of the patient's nostrils using your thumb and place the blade underneath the nose, asking the patient to breathe in and out whilst observing for condensation on the blade. If condensation forms, the nostril that you have not blocked is patent. To observe for alar collapse, block one of the patient's nostrils with your thumb and ask him/her to breathe in very quickly.

Common OSCE cases

Nasal polyps

Symptoms are watery anterior rhinorrhoea, purulent post-nasal drip, nasal obstruction, change in voice and taste and anosmia. Polyps most commonly affect men over 40 years of age and children with cystic fibrosis.

Chronic sinusitis

Symptoms include post-nasal drip, a blocked nose and a foul taste in the mouth. Examination may reveal congested turbinates, infected mucus and polyps.

Tumour

Fractured nose

Key investigations

Endoscopic examination (referral to an ENT surgeon)

HEARING

You are a PRHO in general practice. Mr Arnold is a 63-year-old gentleman who is presenting with difficulty hearing with his left ear. Please assess his hearing. You should take a brief history and perform an examination.

Introduces self and seeks permission to take a history and examine
Confirms patient's name and age

 ## History

Establishes onset and duration of hearing loss
Establishes whether patient has had previous ENT surgery
Establishes whether one or both ears are affected
Establishes whether hearing loss is to high-pitched or low-pitched sounds
Establishes severity of hearing loss and impact on patient's life
Enquires about associated symptoms – vertigo and tinnitus, discharge, loss of balance, pain
Enquires about possible causal factors – noise exposure, treatment with ototoxic drugs, family history
Asks if patient is currently in any pain

 ## Examination

Tests hearing in each ear using speech
Performs the Rinne test using a 512 Hz tuning fork
Performs the Weber test using a 512 Hz tuning fork
Inspects outer ears and behind the ears for any abnormalities and surgical scars
Holds otoscope and patient's ear correctly
Inspects ear canals (otitis externa, wax)
Inspects tympanic membranes and identifies normal anatomy

Cleans hands by washing or using alcohol gel

 ## Global marks

Fluency of examination
Competence in presenting findings, summarizing and forming differential diagnoses

KEY TIPS ⊶●

If a history is required, you should enquire about common causal factors of hearing loss, namely noise exposure and treatment with ototoxic drugs (ask if they have ever had a serious infection requiring intravenous antibiotics); and ask about any family history of hearing loss – a positive history might be suggestive of Meniére's disease.

To test hearing using speech, press on the tragus of one ear to block it off and quietly whisper three numbers into the other ear, asking the patient to repeat them. If the patient is unable to hear the numbers, repeat them with a slightly louder whisper and then normal voice. Practise the tuning fork tests and make sure you are confident at interpreting them. When examining the tympanic membrane with an otoscope you should be able to identify and describe normal anatomy. Abnormalities such as an effusion, inflammation, scarring, perforations and grommets are harder to recognize clearly, so don't worry too much if you struggle. A mannequin head may be used for you to perform otoscopy and identify pathology.

Common OSCE cases

Acoustic neuroma

Commonly presents as ipsilateral tinnitus with or without sensorineural deafness. The Vth and VIIth cranial nerves and cerebellar function may also be affected.

Conductive hearing loss

This may be due to obstruction of the external canal, perforation of the drum due to infection or trauma, or pathology of the ossicular chain due to otosclerosis or infection.

Sensorineural hearing loss

Commonly caused by ototoxic drugs, infection (for example mumps, herpes and meningitis), presbycousis, an acoustic neuroma and multiple sclerosis. Meniére's disease is also a cause of sensorineural deafness and other features of it may be vertigo, nausea and vomiting and tinnitus.

Key investigations

Audiology referral, MRI scan if acoustic neuroma is suspected

DERMATOLOGY

You are a PRHO in general practice. Mrs Lewis is a 40-year-old lady who is complaining of a rash she has had for some time. Please take a short history from her and examine her skin.

Introduces self and seeks permission to take a history and examine
Confirms patient's name and age

History

Enquires about onset and duration of rash, establishing whether it has changed over time
Establishes site of rash
Establishes symptoms – itchiness, discharge and pain/tenderness
Enquires about precipitating/relieving factors including previous treatment
Establishes impact of rash on patient and lifestyle
Enquires about allergies
Enquires about any problems with joints
Establishes patient's past medical and drug history
Asks if patient is currently in any pain

Examination

Inspects skin, nails and joints appropriately
Describes any nail/joint pathology
Palpates rash
Describes distribution and morphology of rash

Cleans hands by washing or using alcohol gel

Global marks

Fluency of examination
Competence in presenting findings, summarizing and forming differential diagnoses

KEY TIPS

A major part of this station is correctly describing the rash you see and you will need to be familiar with some basic dermatological terms. You should describe any rash in terms of its site, colour, size, shape and surface. Some useful terms are listed below.

Site. Describe its exact position if localized. If it is a generalized rash, describe
whether its distribution is flexural or on the extensor aspect of joints, as appropriate.
Colour:
erythematous – suggests increased perfusion
purpuric
salmon-pink.
Shape/size:
plaque – flat-topped disc
macule – flat area of discolouration
papule – an area of elevated skin less than 1 cm in size
nodule – a palpable mass of greater than 1 cm in size.
Surface:
vesicle – blister less than 5 mm in size
bulla – blister greater than 5 mm in size
pustule – a blister containing pus
scale – flaky keratin
crust – dried exudate.

Common OSCE cases

Psoriasis

This can affect the nails and joints as well as skin. Look for pitting, ridging, onycholysis, hyperkeratosis and discolouration of the nails. Psoriasis usually results in salmon-pink plaques with white/silver scaling, and these plaques are found typically on the extensor surfaces of the hands and elbows, the scalp, navel and natal cleft. If you have been presented with a case of psoriasis affecting the hands, ask to look at these other areas. It can also affect the skin by causing guttate or pustular lesions. Psoriatic arthropathy can present in three forms: there may be swelling of the DIP joints, a rheumatoid pattern of disease with symmetrical swelling of small joints, or arthritis mutilans. It can also be associated with ankylosing spondylitis and sacro-iliitis. Differential diagnoses should include a fungal infection, mycosis fungoides and seborrhoeic dermatitis, which may indeed co-exist.

Eczema

Your history may reveal trigger factors such as food or stress. It usually affects the skin in flexural areas, and commonly results in pruritus, excoriation, erythema and fine scaling. When chronic, the lesions may become cracked, lichenified and secondarily infected.

Key investigations
Skin swabs, biopsies and bloods as appropriate

SECTION 3:
EMERGENCY SITUATIONS:
FOCUSED HISTORY AND
MANAGEMENT

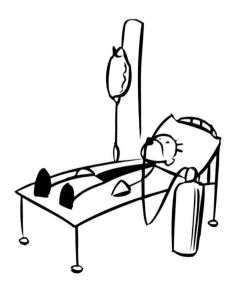

SECTION 3: EMERGENCY SITUATIONS: FOCUSED HISTORY AND MANAGEMENT

In these stations, you will be faced with an acute medical or surgical presentation replicating a typical accident and emergency (A&E) department scenario, and your task is to take a succinct and appropriate history, to aid you in forming a differential diagnosis and management plan. The history needs to be focused due to both the constraints of time in this station and the need for urgent treatment. What you will therefore need to elicit is the history of the presenting complaint, *relevant* past medical history, drug and allergy history, and *relevant* social history, which is usually a smoking and alcohol history. As you are only eliciting information that will assist you to form a differential diagnosis and immediate management plan, family history and housing information are usually not required.

These stations require you to have a sound knowledge of the presentation of common medical and surgical conditions, and this information is most usefully organized into lists of differential diagnoses for common symptom presentations. Thus, if your role-player is presenting with shortness of breath, you will draw on your list of common causes of shortness of breath, and the object of your history will be to narrow down which one of these may be the diagnosis (clinical reasoning). To exemplify, the differential diagnoses of shortness of breath are pulmonary oedema/congestive cardiac failure (CCF), chest infection, pulmonary embolism and chronic obstructive pulmonary disease (COPD)/asthma. The following questions will help you determine which of these is the most likely diagnosis.

Can you tell me about your shortness of breath?
What are you doing when you become short of breath?
How far can you walk before you become short of breath?
Have you had any pain in your chest?
Is your shortness of breath worse when you are lying flat? How many pillows do you sleep on?
Do your ankles swell up? Has this got worse recently?
Have you had any recent surgery? Have you been on a long flight recently?
Have you had a cough recently? Are you coughing anything up?
Have you been feeling feverish?
Are you wheezy when you are short of breath?

You need not ask all the above questions; it might be apparent after the first couple what the most likely diagnosis is. Let the age and sex of the patient inform your diagnosis, as well as any clues at the scene, for example the way the role-player is behaving or inhalers by the bed-side! Drug and past medical history can also be useful, for example in the above scenario the patient may reveal to you that she is taking the oral contraceptive pill (pulmonary embolus) or has a long history of emphysema (exacerbation of COPD). Normally in objective structured clinical examinations (OSCEs), classic presentations are given and all the information the role-player provides you with will usually fit together into an obvious diagnosis.

Your history-taking technique is important in this station, and you will need to find the most effective way for you to take a succinct history. This will involve a combination of open and closed questions, and the balance will vary from person to person. Remember, the role-player is there to help you and will be unlikely to ramble in the way that real patients sometimes do! However, if you find that your 'patient' is giving you a slightly distracted history, you should say something like 'Thank you for that information. I'd like to come back to that later if you don't mind, but right now I really need to ask you a few other questions'. At the end of your history it is always worth asking the role-player if there is anything else he/she would like to tell you that might be relevant – real gems of information can be revealed, especially if you have good rapport with the role-player!

Once you have completed your history, you will need to explain to the 'patient' (or, in some OSCEs, the examiner) what you think the diagnosis might be, and also what your immediate management plan is. In some OSCEs, the examiner will inform you of physical examination findings once you have completed your history, making the situation a bit more real. Management really just means what will you do next, and should include a full examination, any immediate medical management, investigations and senior review.

Learning the management for each medical and surgical emergency may seem daunting, and rather than memorizing a list of management steps for each one you may find it easier to learn the approach. Essentially, immediate medical management is commonly oxygen, intravenous (i.v.) fluids and analgesia as appropriate; and routine investigations in the A&E setting are blood glucose monitoring, urine dipstix testing, arterial blood gas sampling, electrocardiogram (ECG), bloods, blood cultures and X-rays as appropriate. An early request for senior assistance tells the examiner you realize both the gravity of the situation and your own limitations.

Examiner global scores in these stations are for an accurate and succinct history, good history-taking technique (appropriate use of open, closed and clarifying questions), correct differential diagnoses and an appropriate management plan. The role-player will be assessing your rapport and interaction with him or her, including your response to his/her illness and questions and concerns. To prepare for this station you need to become familiar with common acute medical and surgical presentations, and this is best done going on-take and clerking patients, as well as referring to books. We have included some of the common topics for focused history stations in this chapter, and you should practise these as well as use them to familiarize yourself with the approach. You can of course write more stations for further practice. You will need a candidate, an 'examiner' and a role-player whilst using these mark-sheets. The sections entitled 'Key tips' will provide the role-player with information for the history and the 'examiner' with physical examination findings to present to the candidate at the end of the history.

DIABETIC KETOACIDOSIS

You are a medical pre-registration house officer (PRHO) in A&E. Sarah, a 24-year-old office worker, is attending A&E with a day-long history of non-specific abdominal pain and vomiting. She is hyperventilating and has dry mucous membranes. Her observations are as follows: temperature 37 °C, pulse rate 80 beats per minute (bpm), blood pressure 120/75 mmHg, respiratory rate 25 breaths/minute, oxygen saturation 99 per cent in room air. Please take a history and form an appropriate management plan.

 ## History

Makes appropriate introduction
Confirms patient's name and age
Establishes presenting complaint
Explores presenting complaint and asks appropriate follow-up questions
Enquires about past medical history
Establishes drug and allergy history
Enquires about smoking and alcohol consumption

 ## Management

Offers physical examination
Makes appropriate interpretation from history
States intention to check capillary glucose
States intention to obtain i.v. access and start fluid resuscitation
Suggests taking blood for full blood count (FBC), venous glucose, urea, creatinine, electrolytes, liver function tests (LFTs), amylase, bicarbonate and osmolality
States intention to take blood for blood cultures and to dipstix test the urine
Suggests a urine dipstix test and sending urine for microscopy and culture
States intention to request a chest X-ray
States intention to perform an arterial blood gas
Suggests catheterizing the patient
States need to give insulin
Suggests urgent senior review
Discusses implications for patient's long-term management

 ## Global marks

Examiner global rating
Role-player global rating

KEY TIPS ⚯

This is one of the more difficult focused history and management stations and relies on you knowing the various ways in which diabetic ketoacidosis (DKA) can present. Initially the symptoms of abdominal pain and vomiting might suggest a surgical abdomen to you, and therefore appropriate systemic enquiry would be to establish:

the length of the history
the site, nature and severity of the pain
whether the pain radiates anywhere
what the relieving/exacerbating factors are
if there has been any change in bowel habit
a history of the vomiting
a menstrual/contraceptive history
if there are any urinary symptoms

Remember to ask her if there is anything else she wants to mention which might be relevant. Your systemic enquiry will reveal to you that, in addition to the non-specific abdominal pain and vomiting, Sarah is also feeling very lethargic, has had a recent cold and is experiencing polydipsia and polyuria. Past medical and drug history will reveal that Sarah is a known type I diabetic on insulin. Your examiner will inform you that physical examination reveals a soft abdomen, which is mildly tender all over. Bowel sounds and digital rectal examination are unremarkable.

You need only outline the initial steps of the management of DKA and state that Sarah's diabetic management will need reviewing once her condition is stabilized.

HYPOGLYCAEMIA

You are a medical PRHO in A&E. Simon is an 18-year-old student who has been brought to A&E following a single episode of fitting. He looks sweaty and pale, is on 24 per cent oxygen but is otherwise stable. His observations are as follows: pulse rate 95 bpm, blood pressure 120/80 mmHg, respiratory rate 15 breaths/min, and saturations 99 per cent in 24 per cent oxygen. Please take a history and form an appropriate management plan.

 History

Makes appropriate introduction
Confirms patient's name and age
Checks for confusion
Establishes presenting complaint
Explores presenting complaint and asks appropriate follow-up questions
Enquires about past medical history
Establishes drug and allergy history
Enquires about smoking and alcohol consumption

 Management

Offers full physical examination, including a neurological examination
Makes appropriate interpretation from history
States intention to check capillary glucose
States intention to obtain i.v. access
Suggests taking blood for venous glucose, urea, creatinine and electrolytes, calcium, LFTs, and FBC
Suggests giving oral sugar and a longer acting starch, for example toast
Suggests senior review
Discusses implications for patient's longer term management

 Global marks

Examiner global rating
Role-player global rating

KEY TIPS ⚮

This is again one of the harder focused history and management stations, as it relies on you knowing the various ways in which hypoglycaemia can present. Initially your focus will be the reported fitting and therefore appropriate systemic enquiry would be to establish:

loss of consciousness, tongue biting or urinary/faecal incontinence
whether the seizure was witnessed and how it was described
how Simon felt prior to and immediately after the fit
past history of seizures
history of any head injury
history of recent illness
how Simon got to hospital.

Your exploration of the history will reveal that Simon is a newly diagnosed diabetic and has been commenced on insulin treatment by his general practitioner (GP). His medical history is otherwise unremarkable; he has been well recently and he denies any previous history of fitting. He reveals to you that his friends noticed him to be irritable, pale and sweaty prior to trembling and then fitting. He remembers feeling light-headed and a bit faint prior to the fit. He denies tongue biting, loss of consciousness and urinary/faecal incontinence. The examiner will reveal to you that his physical examination is entirely unremarkable. Your interpretation should be that this episode of fitting is most likely to be a presentation of hypoglycaemia, knowing that you will not have been given a history of diabetes if it was not relevant, and hence your management plan is along these lines.

You should state that Simon's diabetic management will need reviewing once his condition has been stabilized.

ACUTE PANCREATITIS

You are a surgical PRHO in A&E. Mr Wykes is a 29-year-old male who is presenting with a 5-day history of vomiting and epigastric pain. Today the pain is much worse. His observations are as follows: pulse rate 95 bpm, blood pressure 110/85 mmHg, oxygen saturation 98 per cent in air, temperature 38.5 °C and respiratory rate 20 breaths/min. Please take a history and form an immediate management plan.

History

Makes appropriate introduction
Confirms patient's name and age
Establishes presenting complaint
Explores presenting complaint and asks appropriate follow-up questions
Enquires about past medical history
Establishes drug and allergy history
Enquires about smoking and alcohol consumption

Management

Offers full examination
States intention to check capillary glucose
States intention to give analgesia
Suggests taking blood for FBC, urea, creatinine and electrolytes, LFTs, lactate dehydrogenase and aspartate transaminase, amylase, C-reactive protein (CRP), calcium, clotting, group and save and venous glucose
States intention to cannulate, and start i.v. hydration
States intention to perform an arterial blood gas
Suggests a urine dipstix test and sending urine for microscopy and culture
States intention to request an erect chest X-ray and plain abdominal film
Suggests keeping the patient nil by mouth
States intention to prescribe compression stockings and prophylactic low molecular weight heparin
States intention to request an ECG
Suggests an ultrasound scan
States intention to ask for senior review

Global marks

Examiner global rating
Role-player global rating

KEY TIPS

The history you will need to elicit in this station is essentially the same as that for any acute abdominal presentation. With reference to pain, you should gain information about:

site,
onset and duration,
nature (e.g. sharp, dull, burning),
severity (is this the worst pain he/she has ever had?),
whether it is constant or intermittent,
radiation,
aggravating and relieving factors (wanting to lie absolutely still suggests peritonitis, wanting to move suggests a colicky pain),
relation to meals, especially spicy/fatty foods,
previous episodes.
Associated features to enquire about are:
nausea and vomiting,
change or abnormality of bowel motions (diarrhoea, constipation and mucus or blood per rectum),
when bowels were last open,
urinary symptoms,
fever,
vaginal discharge, and menstrual and contraceptive history in females.

An ECG is required to exclude cardiac pain presenting as abdominal pain. As part of your pre-operative preparation you should establish when the patient last ate and drank and take blood to group and save. Physiological insults such as the acute abdomen can put the body into a prothrombotic state. This, coupled with likely immobility, requires prophylaxis for venous thromboembolic disease.

Your exploration of the history will reveal that Mr Wykes has severe epigastric pain radiating to the back, eased partially by sitting forward. He has been vomiting stomach contents, and is a heavy drinker. He has had bouts of epigastric pain before, although he has not needed to come to hospital. He has no other significant history. On examination, he is tender in the right upper quadrant with guarding and rebound. The examination is otherwise unremarkable. Your most likely diagnosis is acute pancreatitis.

The common differential diagnoses of epigastric pain are pancreatitis, gastritis, peptic ulcer disease/perforation, biliary colic/cholecystitis/acute cholangitis, acute coronary syndrome, and ruptured/dissecting aortic aneurysm.

CHEST PAIN

You are a medical PRHO in A&E. Mr Starling, a 50-year-old overweight gentleman, is complaining of severe chest pain. He looks pale and sweaty and his observations are as follows: temperature 36 °C, blood pressure 100/65 mmHg, pulse rate 60 bpm, respiratory rate 15 breaths/min and oxygen saturation 90 per cent in room air. Please take a history and form an immediate management plan.

 ## History

Makes appropriate introduction
Confirms patient's name and age
Establishes main symptom
Explores symptom and asks appropriate follow-up questions
Enquires about past medical history
Enquires about family history of arterial disease
Establishes drug and allergy history
Enquires about smoking and alcohol consumption

 ## Management

Offers full examination
Suggests commencing patient on 24 per cent oxygen
States intention to request an ECG
Suggests cardiac monitoring
States intention to gain i.v. access
Suggests commencing immediate drug therapy for acute coronary syndrome: aspirin 300 mg stat., glyceryl trinitrate (GTN) spray, subcutaneous low molecular weight heparin, diamorphine 2.5–5 mg i.v. with 10 mg metoclopramide if required, and GTN infusion if required and systolic blood pressure >100 mmHg
Suggests taking blood for FBC, urea, creatinine and electrolytes, LFTs and amylase (to exclude an abdominal cause), CRP, creatinine kinase, clotting, venous glucose, and a troponin 12 hours post-onset of pain
States intention to take an arterial blood gas
Suggests a chest X-ray
Suggests senior review

Global marks

Examiner global rating
Role-player global rating

KEY TIPS

The common differential diagnoses for chest pain are acute coronary syndrome, musculoskeletal chest pain, chest infection, aortic dissection, an acute abdominal presentation, gastro-oesophageal reflux disease and pulmonary embolism. Below is a list of appropriate follow-up questions that will help ascertain which of these causes may be the diagnosis. As stated in the chapter introduction, you need not ask all these questions, just enough to establish the diagnosis in your own mind. You could also ask an open question such as 'Can you tell me about your pain?' and see what information is volunteered before asking more specific, closed questions.

Did the pain come on suddenly or gradually?
What were you doing when the pain came on?
How long have you had the pain for?
Is the pain central or located to one side?
What is the nature of the pain (heavy, crushing, sharp, burning)?
How severe is the pain on a scale of 1 to 10 (10 being the most severe)?
Are you short of breath with the chest pain?
Do you feel nauseous? Have you vomited?
Do you feel sweaty?
Do you feel the pain or any tingling in your left arm, neck or jaw?
Has anything relieved the pain (maybe GTN in the ambulance!)?
Have you had a pain like this before?
Is it worse on breathing in or coughing (pleuritic chest pain)?
Is it related to position?
Have you had a cough/fever?
Have been abroad recently or had any surgery?
Have you hurt or injured your chest in any way?
Is it related to meals?

In your exploration of the history you learn that Mr Starling had a sudden episode of chest pain at rest. It was central chest pain, heavy in nature and very severe. He vomited once with the pain and became very sweaty. The pain was associated with left arm tingling and was relieved by the GTN spray given to him by the ambulance crew. He is a known hypertensive on medication and is a smoker. He has no other significant history. Physical examination is entirely normal. Your diagnosis is that Mr Starling has had an acute cardiac event and your management should be as such.

The management described opposite is for an acute coronary syndrome; you should also know the management of the other common causes of chest pain.

SHORTNESS OF BREATH

You are a medical PRHO in A&E. Mr Jones, an elderly gentleman, is acutely short of breath. His observations are as follows: temperature 37.5 °C, blood pressure 120/80 mmHg, pulse rate 75 bpm, respiratory rate 25 breaths/min, oxygen saturation 93 per cent in 28 per cent oxygen. Please take a history and form an immediate management plan.

 ## History

Makes appropriate introduction
Confirms patient's name and age
Establishes main symptom
Explores symptom and asks appropriate follow-up questions
Enquires about past medical history
Establishes drug and allergy history
Enquires about smoking and alcohol consumption
Enquires about employment history (asbestos exposure, bird keeping etc.)

 ## Management

Offers full examination
States intention to start oxygen therapy at appropriate flow rate
Suggests a chest X-ray
Suggests an ECG
Suggests taking blood for FBC, urea, creatinine and electrolytes, CRP, d-dimer and a troponin (if appropriate)
States intention to perform an arterial blood gas
States intention to gain i.v. access and, if appropriate, commence i.v. hydration
Suggests commencing drug therapy as appropriate: nebulizers, i.v. hydrocortisone, i.v. frusemide, low molecular weight heparin, i.v. GTN infusion, antibiotics, and paracetamol if pyrexial
Suggests senior review

 ## Global marks

Examiner global rating
Role-player global rating

KEY TIPS

The common differential diagnoses for shortness of breath are chest infection, pulmonary oedema, acute asthma attack, acute exacerbation of COPD, pulmonary embolism and pneumothorax. Below is a list of appropriate follow-up questions that will help you distinguish which of these causes is the diagnosis.

When do you become short of breath?
Have you had problems with your breathing before?
Do you ever have pain in your chest?
Do your ankles swell up?
Do you get short of breath when lying flat?
How many pillows do you sleep on at night?
How far can you walk before you become short of breath?
Do you get wheezy?
Do you have a cough?
Are you coughing anything up? If so, what colour is it?
Have you been feeling feverish?
Have you been on a long flight recently?
Do you use the oral contraceptive pill (if female)?
Have you had any recent surgery?

In your exploration of the history, you learn that Mr Jones has a long-standing history of COPD for which he is normally on inhalers. He has had a cough productive of yellow-green sputum for a few days and has been feverish. He is a life-long smoker but does not drink alcohol. On examination he has widespread wheeze in both lung fields, and bronchial breathing and coarse crackles at the right lung base. Your working diagnosis is that Mr Jones is suffering an infective exacerbation of his COPD, and you should manage him accordingly.

STRANGULATED INGUINAL HERNIA

Mr Hicks is a 75-year-old gentleman who lives in a residential home. His GP has referred him to A&E for a swelling in his groin that is associated with pain and vomiting. As the surgical PRHO, you have been asked to clerk him. Please take a focused history and form an immediate management plan. His observations are as follows: pulse rate 90 bpm, blood pressure 157/95 mmHg, oxygen saturation 97 per cent in room air, respiratory rate 18 breaths/min, temperature 38.5 °C.

 ## History

Makes appropriate introduction
Confirms patient's name and age
Establishes main presenting symptom
Explores symptom and asks appropriate follow-up questions
Enquires about past medical history
Establishes drug and allergy history
Enquires about smoking and alcohol consumption

 ## Management

Offers a full examination
States intention to gain i.v. access and commence i.v. fluids
States intention to prescribe analgesia and anti-emetics
States intention to prescribe compression stockings (after excluding arterial disease) and a prophylactic dose of a low molecular weight heparin
Suggests keeping patient nil by mouth and states intention to pass a nasogastric tube
Suggests taking blood for FBC, urea, creatinine and electrolytes, LFTs, clotting and group and save
States intention to request a plain abdominal X-ray and an erect chest X-ray
Suggests a urine dipstix test
Suggests requesting a pre-operative ECG
Suggests urgent senior review

Global marks

Examiner global rating
Role-player global rating

KEY TIPS ⚎

You should know the difference between reducible, incarcerated and strangulated hernias (the latter two both being irreducible) and their associated symptoms. You should also know the differential diagnoses of a groin swelling. The following questions will aid you in establishing whether a hernia is reducible, incarcerated or strangulated.

How long has the swelling been there?
Does it hurt? (Pain suggests strangulation.)
What is the nature of the pain?
Where is the pain?
How severe is the pain on a scale of 1 to 10 (10 being the most severe)?
Does anything make the pain better or worse?
Can you push the swelling in?
Have you lost your appetite?
Do you feel nauseous?
Are you vomiting?
Are you opening your bowels normally? (If there has not been a bowel motion, you should ask if the patient is passing flatus.)

The last few questions are assessing for symptoms of bowel obstruction. A strangulated hernia is a surgical emergency and will require an emergency laparotomy – ask your patient if he/she has ever had a general anaesthetic before, and also when he/she last ate or drank.

Your exploration of the history reveals that Mr Hicks has had the groin swelling for some time but is unsure how long. He last opened his bowels 3 days ago and is vomiting up any food or drink he has. He has had no previous surgery and is a known hypertensive and diabetic on medication. On examination his abdomen is distended, and his groin swelling is very tender and irreducible. He has tinkling bowel sounds. The examination is otherwise unremarkable. Your diagnosis is that Mr Hicks has a strangulated inguinal hernia and you should manage him as such.

ECTOPIC PREGNANCY

You are a surgical PRHO in A&E. Miss Mackintosh is a young woman complaining of severe lower abdominal pain. Her observations are as follows: temperature 38 °C, blood pressure 125/75 mmHg, pulse rate 130 bpm, oxygen saturation 98 per cent in air. Please take a short history and form an immediate management plan.

History

Makes appropriate introduction
Confirms patient's name and age
Establishes main symptom
Explores symptom and asks appropriate follow-up questions
Enquires about past medical history
Establishes drug and allergy history
Enquires about smoking and alcohol consumption

Management

Offers full examination, including a vaginal examination
States intention to take blood for FBC, urea, creatinine and electrolytes, LFTs, amylase, clotting screen, group and save (cross-match and rhesus status if suspected ectopic pregnancy rupture), serum save for possible beta-human chorionic gonadotrophin (β-hCG) and progesterone measurement
Suggests gaining i.v. access and commencing i.v. hydration
Suggests keeping patient nil by mouth
States intention to give analgesia and anti-emetics as required
States intention to request a urine dipstix test, and urinary β-hCG test
Suggests an urgent ultrasound scan
Suggests senior review

Global marks

Examiner global rating
Role-player global rating

KEY TIPS 🔑

The common differential diagnoses of lower abdominal pain in a young woman are appendicitis, renal colic, ectopic pregnancy, other pregnancy-related causes, pelvic inflammatory disease, ovarian cyst pathology, urinary tract infection and inflammatory bowel disease. The following questions will help you decide which of these is the correct diagnosis.

Where is the pain?
How long have you had the pain?
How severe is the pain on a score of 1 to 10 (10 being the most severe)?
What is the nature of the pain?
Does the pain go anywhere else?
Does anything make the pain better or worse?
Is the pain related to eating or moving your bowels?
Do you feel hungry?
Do you feel nauseous? Have you vomited?
Has there been a change in bowel habit? When did you last open your bowels?
Are you pressing any blood or mucous from the back passage?
Have you had any pain on passing urine or any other change in your urine?
When was your last menstrual period?
Is there a possibility of pregnancy?
Have you had any vaginal discharge or bleeding?
Do you experience pain on deep sexual intercourse?

On exploration of the history you learn that it is a left-sided lower abdominal pain that has been there for 1 day. Miss Mackintosh has been vomiting, usually when the pain is at its most severe. It is a sharp pain, and there are no bowel or urinary symptoms. Her last menstrual period was 6 weeks ago, which is unusual for her, and she admits to the possibility of pregnancy. Examination reveals localized abdominal tenderness with guarding in the left iliac fossa. Her digital rectal and vaginal examinations are unremarkable. You are unable to palpate her uterus. You suspect that she has an ectopic pregnancy and you should manage her as such.

SECTION 4:
DISCHARGE PLANNING

SECTION 4: DISCHARGE PLANNING

This chapter includes three slightly different types of objective structured clinical examination (OSCE) station, all of which are related to discharging a patient home after an inpatient stay. The first of these is about discharging a patient home with long-term drug therapy, and we have used steroid therapy as an example. There are several aspects of long-term drug therapy that ought to be conveyed to patients before discharging them into the community, to aid compliance and pharmacological efficacy and safety. For better compliance, you need to ensure that your patient understands why the treatment has been started, and indeed why it needs to be continued. For pharmacological efficacy and safety, patients should be aware of any important side effects and their presentation, as well as common drug interactions. They should also be made aware of any follow-up that will be arranged to monitor disease progress and drug therapy. Although steroid therapy has been used as an example, a similar station could be written about any long-term drug therapy and another good example would be discharging a patient home on warfarin. The mark-sheet for a warfarin station would be slightly different, and would also include explaining the need for regular blood tests, explaining the interaction with excessive alcohol and giving advice about traumatic activity such as contact sports. As for all sections, use these mark-sheets as a guide to write and practise many more; all you need to do is think about what you would want to be told about a particular treatment if you were the patient.

The second type of station is about addressing the social issues surrounding the discharge of an elderly patient home, a scenario which will become very familiar to you once you start working as a doctor. It is a complex process, and a good way to gain insight into it is by attending an elderly care multi-disciplinary team meeting.

Finally, the third type of station is about discharging a patient home after a major illness. The example here is about discharge after a myocardial infarction (MI); however, for practice you can write mark-sheets referring to any major illness, those for which treatment will need to be continued and lifestyle changes made being the most suitable. Some examples are chronic obstructive pulmonary disease, alcohol-related pancreatitis, cerebrovascular disease and epilepsy. You will mostly be aware of lifestyle modifications and sensible follow-up arrangements for major illnesses. However, you may not be familiar with advice on recommencing work and activities such as driving. You could look at some patient leaflets to gain more information about this, but if you are not sure, just say to the 'patient' that there may be some short-term lifestyle implications that you are not entirely sure of, and that you will find out and let him/her know. This will tell the examiner that you are aware that patients need to be given information about when it is safe to recommence everyday activities. Generally, in all stations, if the 'patient' asks you a question about which you are not sure, don't be frightened to admit this and tell him/her that you will endeavour to find out; global marks are allocated for your rapport and conduct as much as they are for your medical knowledge.

DISCHARGING A PATIENT ON STEROID THERAPY

Mrs Potter, a 61-year-old lady, is to be discharged home following an acute admission for a flare of her rheumatoid arthritis. She is to be discharged home on a long course of steroids and, as the medical pre-registration house officer (PRHO), you have been asked to discuss the important aspects of steroid therapy with her.

Gives appropriate introduction of self and states the purpose of the interview
Confirms patient's name and age
Checks patient's understanding of the current situation – admission diagnosis and treatment given in hospital
Checks that the patient feels ready to go home
Explains the danger of suddenly stopping steroid therapy
Explains the risk of intercurrent infection
Explains the possible effect on blood pressure and blood glucose levels
Discusses the effect of bone thinning and osteoporosis, and explains bisphosphonate prophylaxis
Discusses the gastrointestinal side effects, and explains cover with a proton pump inhibitor
Warns of increased appetite and potential weight gain
Warns of skin thinning and risk of bruising
Explains to the patient why a steroid bracelet must be worn at all times
Ensures that the patient has a steroid card and discusses what it is for
Informs patient that she will be followed-up in the rheumatology clinic
Addresses the patient's questions and concerns

 ## Global marks

Examiner global rating
Role-player global rating

KEY TIPS ⚬━●

A good way of starting this station is to explain to the 'patient' that she has been started on steroids, and then to ask her if she knows anything about steroids. By doing this you will address any misconceptions or concerns from the outset, and you will know which aspects you need to explore in some depth and which you can merely mention to score the point on the mark-sheet.

It is helpful to ask the 'patient' if she has been given a steroid card, as the role-player may produce one in the OSCE, allowing you to use it as a prompt! The steroid card provides guidance to the patient on minimizing risk, and details of the prescriber, drug, dose and duration of treatment for the benefit of other health professionals.

You must explain to the 'patient' why it is necessary for her to wear a steroid bracelet, and take the time to reassure her that her progress and any side effects will be monitored.

The examiner global marks in this station are for your knowledge of the drug therapy and the clarity and appropriateness with which you deliver this information. The role-player will assess your communication of medical information from a patient's perspective.

DISCHARGING AN ELDERLY PATIENT HOME

You are a surgical PRHO. Your team had admitted Mrs Abrahams, an 87-year-old, frail lady with sub-acute bowel obstruction, which has now resolved. She is ready to go home and you have been asked to assess her home situation to help form plans for discharge.

Gives appropriate introduction of self and states the purpose of the interview
Confirms patient's name and age
Establishes patient's understanding of her current medical problems
Checks that the patient is aware that discharge is imminent, and ensures that she is happy with this
Acknowledges patient's concerns and answers any questions

Assesses home situation

Asks if the patient lives alone
Establishes the type of housing
Establishes whether the patient managed independently prior to admission, or whether there was input from social services, a district nurse or anyone else

Makes appropriate plan

Asks if the patient would like to have input from social services
Informs the patient that she will be seen by a physiotherapist and an occupational therapist prior to discharge
Gives appropriate medical information
States intention to contact the general practitioner
Makes a sensible plan for follow-up

Global marks

Examiner global rating
Role-player global rating

KEY TIPS 🔑

A good way to assess whether someone is happy to be discharged is to ask if he or she is keen to get home and return to normal activity. Be tactful when enquiring about whether someone lives alone; a phrase that proves quite useful is 'Is anyone at home with you?'.

The sort of assistance that social services commonly provides is meals-on-wheels, day centres and carers to assist with personal care, food and drink preparation and domestic tasks. The physiotherapist is involved to ensure that the patient's mobility is good enough for discharge home, and the occupational therapist ensures that the patient is safe with activities of daily living and may make a home visit to ensure the safety of the home environment.

In this station you need to demonstrate a holistic approach and a clear understanding of all the issues with regard to discharge planning for elderly patients. You should also demonstrate an understanding of the primary/secondary care interface. Your focus is therefore not on the medical aspects of discharge, but you should give brief advice on any treatment the 'patient' will be discharged on, and what follow-up arrangements will be made.

DISCHARGING A PATIENT HOME AFTER A MAJOR ILLNESS

You are a medical PRHO. Your firm is discharging Mr Hindes, a 56-year-old gentleman who had been admitted for an acute MI. Please discuss with Mr Hindes how he can minimize his cardiovascular risk, when he can re-start everyday activities and what the treatment and follow-up plans are.

Gives appropriate introduction of self and states the purpose of the interview
Confirms patient's name and age
Checks that the patient feels ready to be discharged
Establishes patient's understanding of the diagnosis, and investigations and treatment that have taken place in hospital
Enquires about smoking, and gives appropriate advice
Gives dietary advice
Gives exercise advice
Acknowledges patient's concerns, and answers questions appropriately
Explains what treatment will be continued on discharge
Gives advice about resuming driving and starting work
Makes a sensible plan for follow-up

Global marks

Examiner global rating
Role-player rating

KEY TIPS ⚊●

Again, the best way to start this station is to ascertain what understanding the 'patient' already has, thus enabling you to concentrate on some aspects more than others. Even if the 'patient' has good knowledge of a particular aspect, you must still mention it, perhaps by summarizing what you have heard, or the examiner may not give you the mark for addressing that particular point.

The 'patient's' concerns may be about resuming a normal life and he may want further information about this, for example commencing sexual intercourse or air travel.

Global marks from the examiner will be for your knowledge of lifestyle implications/modifications, on-going treatment and follow-up arrangements. Role-player global marks will be for your handling of his questions/concerns your empathy with his situation and the fluency of your consultation (avoid using medical jargon!).

SECTION 5:
CHRONIC DISEASE
MANAGEMENT

SECTION 5: CHRONIC DISEASE MANAGEMENT

Chronic disease management is a large part of what happens in hospital outpatients and general practice, and these stations are used to assess your knowledge of common conditions and their management, as well as your ability to conduct a patient-focused medical consultation. The basic structure of any chronic disease consultation is the same; however, the specific questions and management will depend on the condition being treated. In this section we outline what a chronic disease consultation should consist of. We have also included mark-sheets for a hypertension station and a diabetes station, which will further clarify and exemplify this. It will be useful to use these mark-sheets as templates to practise other chronic disease management stations, asthma, human immunodeficiency virus infection and heart failure being a few examples. Good places to prepare for these stations are medical outpatients and general practice chronic disease clinics.

The general structure of a chronic disease consultation is outlined below.

- To measure disease control subjectively (patient's view of symptom control).
- To measure disease control objectively (for example a blood pressure reading in hypertension or capillary glucose measurement in diabetes).
- To assess for complications of the disease and end-organ damage.
- To establish occupation, smoking and alcohol histories, and other lifestyle issues such as diet and exercise if appropriate.
- To take a general medical and drug history.
- To enquire about tolerability and side effects of chronic disease drugs, as well as compliance.
- If relevant, to explore why disease control might be poor.
- To decide jointly with the patient about any modification to the treatment.
- To arrange any investigations and follow-up as appropriate.

In order to achieve good examiner global marks you will need to demonstrate a sound knowledge of the chronic disease you are managing, and form a reasonable management plan. Your consultation will need to be fluent; it is best not to look as though you are thinking about what to ask next. The key to good long-term management of a disease is to consider the patient's perspective. The role-player will be assessing how satisfied he or she felt with your consultation in his/her role as a patient. The role-player will be scoring you for your professionalism, whether you dealt adequately with any concerns or difficulties he or she had, and the rapport you established (remember to avoid using medical jargon!).

HYPERTENSION

You are a pre-registration house officer (PRHO) in general practice and you have been asked by the practice nurse to see Mr Patel, a known hypertensive patient. She is concerned that his blood pressure has been poorly controlled, with the last measurement being 190/105 mmHg. Please explore why Mr Patel's blood pressure is poorly controlled, explore any potential complications, and discuss your management plan with Mr Patel.

Gives appropriate introduction and states the purpose of the consultation
Confirms patient's name, age and occupation

Assesses current status

Enquires about general health
Asks to look at self-monitoring results to assess control of hypertension
Enquires about symptoms of hypertension
Enquires about symptoms of hypertensive and organ damage
Establishes duration of hypertension
Explores possible reasons for increase in blood pressure
Enquires about past medical history
Enquires about drug history
Enquires about smoking and alcohol history
Enquires about diet and level of physical activity

Discusses management plan

Explains possible reason for increase in blood pressure to the patient
Discusses the need for change or continuation of the current treatment as appropriate
Explains investigations to be arranged
Plans appropriate follow-up

Global marks

Examiner global rating
Role-player global rating

KEY TIPS ⚬━●

This section includes key tips that are specific to a hypertension chronic disease management station. However, they will give you some idea about the sort of knowledge you will need to have for any chronic disease management station.

Hypertension is rarely symptomatic. However, you ought to enquire about headache, visual disturbance, chest pain and claudication pain, the latter three being symptoms of hypertensive end-organ damage. Your objective measure of disease control will be blood pressure recordings in the patient's medical notes, and any home blood pressure readings.

Reversible causes of hypertension are excessive alcohol consumption, lack of exercise, poor compliance with medication, stress, high dietary salt intake and being overweight. Ask the patient whether he or she is taking his/her medication, as non-compliance may be the cause for the blood pressure remaining elevated. Drug interactions may be contributing to poor blood pressure control, thus a drug history is very important.

Whilst enquiring about past medical history, you should specifically ask about diabetes, ischaemic heart disease, cerebrovascular disease and peripheral vascular disease. This information assists you in risk profiling your patient, an important aspect of chronic disease management. Investigations are also used in this process, so you should request an electrocardiogram (ECG), a chest X-ray and bloods for renal function, plasma lipids and glucose. You would, of course, complete your risk profiling with an examination of the cardiovascular system and the retinae.

Follow-up should be at approximately 2 weeks after a change in treatment has been instigated and, if you are simply monitoring the patient, 2-weekly blood pressure readings for about 6 weeks would be a reasonable follow-up plan.

DIABETES

You are a PRHO in general practice and are seeing Mr Keenan, a 60-year-old man with a long-standing history of type II diabetes mellitus. He has come to you for a diabetes check-up – although he is not yet due for his annual review. Please undertake a review of Mr Keenan's diabetes, and discuss with him what the management plan should be (investigations and follow-up). You will not have time to perform a physical examination; however, you should inform the examiner of what you would like to do.

Gives appropriate introduction
Confirms patient's name, age and occupation
Asks an open question, allowing the patient to state the purpose of his visit

Assesses current status

Enquires about general health
Asks to look at self-monitoring results to assess glycaemic control
Enquires about symptoms of hypoglycaemia and hyperglycaemia
Enquires about symptoms of diabetic complications
Asks about past medical history
Confirms drug history
Enquires about smoking and alcohol history
Enquires about diet and level of physical activity

Informs examiner of planned physical examination

States intention to measure and weigh the patient and calculate the body mass index
States intention to take a blood pressure reading
Suggests assessing distance visual acuity and performing fundoscopy
Suggests an examination of the foot (inspection of the skin and nails, inspection for ulceration or foot deformity, palpation of pedal pulses, assessment of joint vibration sense and pinprick sensation)
Suggests inspection of injection site in insulin-treated patients

Discusses management plan with patient

Discusses a urine dipstix test (proteinuria)
Discusses attending the hospital for fasting blood tests (renal function, haemoglobin A1c, fasting lipid profile)
Makes appropriate plan for follow-up

Global marks

Examiner global rating
Role-player global rating

KEY TIPS ⚯

You could not be expected to perform a full diabetic assessment in a 7-minute station, so read the instructions carefully. However, if your school has longer stations and a full assessment is required, performing all the points opposite will constitute a complete review.

In the scenario opposite, Mr Keenan reveals to you that his best friend, who also has diabetes, has just had a myocardial infarction and this has made him concerned about his own health. The global marks in this station will in part be for your acknowledgement of his concerns, your reassurance by way of performing the assessment and making a further appointment to see him with the results, as well as your ability to conduct a diabetes review.

Common symptoms of hypoglycaemia are hunger, trembling, sweating and dizziness. Symptoms of hyperglycaemia are thirst, tiredness and urinary frequency.

To assess for the complications of diabetes, you need to ask about the following symptoms.

Change in vision (retinopathy).
Chest pain (macrovascular – ischaemic heart disease).
Claudication (macrovascular – peripheral vascular disease).
Numbness and tingling (sensory neuropathy).
Impotence (autonomic neuropathy).

Whilst taking a past medical history, you should ask specifically about ischaemic heart disease, cerebrovascular disease, renal disease, peripheral vascular disease and hypertension. This will help you risk profile your patient and also plan extra investigations (for example ECG or chest X-ray).

Appropriate follow-up would be in 2 weeks, as it usually takes time for blood results to reach general practitioners. If the patient's self-monitoring results were not satisfactory (i.e. blood glucose was running too high or too low), you would ask for a senior review and together consider making changes to the diabetic regime.

SECTION 6:
CONDUCTING AN INTERVIEW WITH PATIENTS WITH MENTAL HEALTH AND COGNITIVE PROBLEMS

SECTION 6: CONDUCTING AN INTERVIEW WITH PATIENTS WITH MENTAL HEALTH AND COGNITIVE PROBLEMS

This chapter embraces a whole group of stations that focus on conducting an interview with patients with mental health problems, cognitive problems, substance misuse or psychological difficulties. In the final year at many medical schools, psychiatry is examined separately from medicine and surgery, and if this is the case at your school, the range of mental health problems you will encounter in a finals objective structured clinical examination (OSCE) will be limited to those for which a psychiatric or psychological problem could be a presentation of a medical condition.

OSCE situations do not allow you the time that you would normally have to carry out a full psychiatric assessment, making psychiatric history taking in an OSCE setting quite difficult. However, you need to accept this limitation and focus on the key aspects of the assessment whilst bearing in mind that in front of you is a role-player, not a real patient! It is not always easy to know which aspects to concentrate on; the station instructions should be your guide and, it is well worth reading them carefully. For example, if the scenario says 'this lady is having some difficulty with her memory and I would like you to perform a mini mental state examination', the focus really is on building a rapport, gaining consent and then doing the mini mental state examination; a full psychiatric assessment is not required.

Commencing your history with an open question should immediately give you clues about the nature of the psychiatric problem you are being presented with, as will your observation of the scene. For example, your 'patient' with low mood might be slumped forward, demonstrating psychomotor retardation, and your 'patient' presenting with psychotic symptoms may be distracted and turning around to listen to his or her auditory hallucinations. If you are struggling with your history, bear in mind that there are several generic questions for which marks are allocated, and it is easy to use these to boost your score. They are enquiries about past psychiatric history, past medical history, family history and social history, which includes questions about alcohol, smoking, occupation and home status. As for any history station, ask your 'patient' at the end of your history if there is anything he/she wants to raise which may be relevant; both in OSCE stations and reality, many gems of information are revealed by this question!

The differential diagnosis of a psychiatric presentation is clearly of one or more psychiatric disorders or an underlying medical problem. Hence in every psychiatric history, although the focus should be on the diagnosis you think most likely, you always need to ask brief screening questions to exclude the other diagnoses. So, for example, if you think that your 'patient' has schizophrenia and he/she has answered in the affirmative to your enquiry about first-rank symptoms, you must still ask about low mood and sleep disturbance to exclude the differential diagnosis of depression. If the 'patient' is tired all the time and you think this is due to depression, don't forget to ask questions that may uncover an underlying medical diagnosis, for example anaemia or hypothyroidism.

In these stations, the examiner global rating marks will be allocated for the ease and fluency with which you conduct your task, its appropriateness and thoroughness, and your summary and differential diagnosis. As always, it is worth practising how to summarize – the following example may help you.

> In summary *(sign-posting!)*, Mrs Jones is a 45-year-old lady who is presenting with a month-long history of low mood, early morning wakening, tearfulness and loss of appetite. She is finding it difficult to conduct her normal activities, but denies suicidal intent. She is otherwise well and has no previous psychiatric history. Her presentation meets the criteria for a diagnosis of depression; however, other possibilities include bipolar disorder, and mood disorder secondary to a medical condition.

The role-player will be marking your rapport, empathy and interaction with him/her as a patient. A demonstration of your verbal and non-verbal communication skills, for example making eye contact, leaning slightly forward, and modifying your tone of voice to express empathy with his/her situation, will boost these marks.

Common OSCE scenarios are low mood, a presentation of psychotic symptoms, tired all the time, alcohol misuse, suicide attempt, impaired cognitive function and anxiety symptoms. Model mark-sheets for some of these follow, but, as always, use these as a guide for writing more for scenarios that have not been included.

COGNITIVE FUNCTION

You are a pre-registration house officer (PRHO) in general practice. Mr Williams, a 78-year-old gentleman, has been brought to the surgery by his daughter. She is concerned that he has become increasingly forgetful and withdrawn. Please take a history to assess his mental state and ask any further questions to help form a differential diagnosis.

Gives appropriate introduction of self
Establishes patient's name, age and occupation
Establishes the patient's reason for attending the surgery
Explains the purpose of the interview
Assesses cognitive function
Screens for depression
Enquires about hallucinations and delusions
Establishes patient's insight
Enquires about past psychiatric history
Asks about general well-being and any change in physical health
Enquires about medical and drug history
Enquires about social history
Suggests a full physical examination and baseline investigations to exclude a medical cause

Global marks

Examiner global rating
Role-player global rating

KEY TIPS 🔑

In reality, assessing an elderly person with this presentation would take a lot longer than a few minutes, and would include a complete medical review as well as an assessment of cognitive and mental state.

You should be familiar with the 10-point and 30-point mini mental tests. However, be careful to follow the instructions for the station – this particular scenario does not require you to perform either of these tests. If the instructions are unclear, it is worth asking the examiner what sort of assessment is required and if either of the mini mental tests should be used.

The following enquiries will provide a quick assessment of the various aspects of cognitive function: orientation (person, time, place), short-term memory (address), long-term memory (date of World War I), concentration (counting backwards from 20) and recognition (naming two common objects). It is useful to introduce your cognitive assessment to the patient by saying something like 'I'd like to ask you some questions to test your memory and concentration. Some of them may seem very easy, but they are just routine questions'.

Your differential diagnoses will be cognitive impairment secondary to a dementing process, depression presenting as pseudodementia, a psychotic illness, or confusion secondary to a medical condition. To help clarify which of these is most likely, you will need to ask screening questions for depression – ask about low mood, anhedonia, sleep disturbance, weight loss and decreased appetite; and also enquire about hallucinations and delusions. If time permits, you could complete the 10-point mini mental test and include the score in your summary – a score of less than 6 is suggestive of impaired cognitive function.

ALCOHOL

You are a PRHO in general practice. You have called back Mr Terry, a 51-year-old gentleman, after noting a raised gamma glutamyl transferase and mean cell volume on some routine blood tests. You suspect that he may be drinking excessive amounts of alcohol. Please take an appropriate history and give advice as necessary.

Gives appropriate introduction of self and states reason for the interview
Confirms patient's name, age and occupation
Establishes patient's quantity of alcohol intake
Establishes pattern of alcohol intake (type, place, time)
Asks CAGE questionnaire (see opposite)
Enquires about physical symptoms secondary to alcohol misuse
Enquires about features of dependence (craving, withdrawal, lessening effect)
Establishes social history and enquires about psychosocial impact of alcohol
Asks about delusions, hallucinations and low mood
Enquires about past psychiatric history
Enquires about past medical history and drug history
Gives appropriate advice about safe drinking levels and cutting down

 ## Global marks

Examiner global rating
Role-player global rating

KEY TIPS —●

Below are some phrases which might be useful in this station.

Take me through an average day's alcohol intake.
Do you drink alone?
(CAGE)
   Have you ever tried to Cut down the amount of alcohol you drink?
   Do you get Angry when people comment on your drinking?
   Do you feel Guilty about the amount of alcohol you drink?
   Do you drink Early in the morning?
Does alcohol have the same effect on you that it used to?

Common physical manifestations of alcohol misuse are nausea, epigastric abdominal pain and arterial disease. Alcohol misuse can impact on relationships and work and can cause financial/legal difficulties, and this information should be elicited as part of a social history. Asking about delusions, hallucinations and low mood is important in establishing whether there may be associated depression, schizophrenia etc. or whether alcohol misuse is the sole problem.

PSYCHOTIC SYMPTOMS

You are a PRHO in general practice. Gary Harris, a 19-year-old student, attends with a friend. His friend is concerned about Gary as he has been behaving a bit strangely over the last few weeks and has been shutting himself in his room for most of the day. Please take an appropriate history from Gary and form a differential diagnosis.

Gives appropriate introduction of self
Confirms patient's name, age and occupation
States the purpose of the interview
Asks an open question, allowing the patient to tell the history
Enquires specifically about thought insertion, broadcasting and withdrawal
Enquires about feelings of passivity
Enquires about persecutory delusions
Enquires about feelings of grandiosity
Enquires about hallucinations
Excludes symptoms of depression
Establishes any psychosocial stressors/life events
Establishes insight
Enquires about past psychiatric history
Enquires about family history
Asks about general well-being and any change in physical health
Establishes medical and drug history
Establishes social history

Global marks

Examiner global rating
Role-player global rating

KEY TIPS

As for all psychiatric history stations, take in the scene and use the role-player's dress and behaviour as clues. If the role-player gives you a cue, for example looking up at the ceiling, ask about it. He/she may reveal to you that there is a voice talking to him/her from the ceiling.

Taking a history about psychotic symptoms can be quite difficult, and below are some questions which may prove useful. Of course they are for guidance only, and you must practise questions that you feel comfortable using.

Gary, I understand that your friend thinks that you've been behaving a bit differently recently. Would you like to tell me what's been going on?
Has anyone been interfering with your thoughts in any way?
Do you feel that something or someone is controlling you?
Do you feel safe at the moment?
Do you feel very important at the moment?
Do you ever hear, smell, see or feel things that you think other people don't?
Do you think that all these things that are happening to you are real, or a bit strange?

Psychotic symptoms are commonly due to schizophrenia, depression, mania or delusional disorder.

LOW MOOD

You are a PRHO in general practice. Mrs Vinnels is a 42-year-old lady who has presented to your surgery feeling 'down in the dumps', and this has been going on for some time. Please take an appropriate history from her and form a differential diagnosis.

Gives appropriate introduction of self
Confirms patient's name, age and occupation
Asks an open question allowing the patient to tell the history
Enquires about depressive cognitions
Enquires about the somatic features of depression
Enquires about psychosocial stressors and life events
Enquires about previous psychiatric history and other psychiatric symptoms
Asks about suicide intent
Asks about general well-being and any change in physical health
Establishes medical and drug history
Asks about family history
Enquires about social history

 ## Global marks

Examiner global rating
Role-player global rating

KEY TIPS 🔑

In depression, the patient suffers from lowering of mood, reduction of energy and a decrease in activity; capacity for enjoyment, interest and concentration is reduced and marked tiredness is common. Self-esteem and self-confidence are often reduced, and ideas of worthlessness and guilt are sometimes present. These features may be accompanied by somatic symptoms:

loss of interest and pleasurable feelings,
waking in the morning earlier than usual,
low mood is worst in the morning (diurnal variation),
marked psychomotor retardation,
agitation,
loss of appetite,
weight loss,
loss of libido.

As for all OSCE history stations, the examiner can give you the marks opposite if you have either asked a series of closed questions or if your use of open questioning and rapport has allowed the 'patient' to reveal all the required information to you. If the latter is the case, summarize the relevant information back to the 'patient', thus demonstrating to the examiner that you know what a depression history includes. It will also demonstrate your ability to summarize and interpret what the 'patient' has said.

Asking about suicidal intent is always difficult, but a good question would be 'Have you felt that things have got so bad that you feel like ending it all?' Of course, practise a question that you will feel comfortable asking.

The common differential diagnoses of low mood are depression, bipolar depression, mood disorder due to a general medical condition, and adjustment disorder following a bereavement or traumatic event (post-traumatic stress disorder). Therefore asking about manic episodes, hallucinations and delusions will help narrow your list of possible diagnoses, as will asking about physical health and psychosocial stress.

SECTION 7:
COMMUNICATION

SECTION 7: COMMUNICATION

Communication scenarios are stations that some candidates easily sail through, and others find very difficult. Most students assume that some people are naturally good at communication scenarios and others simply are not. Whilst this may be true, there is no reason why the required skills cannot be learnt. Like any other type of clinical skill, practice is the key. Most medical schools teach communication skills, but if through your course you missed these sessions, now is the time to start. You may be fortunate enough to find a communications tutor who is willing to facilitate a session for you and a small group of your peers in the run-up to your final objective structured clinical examination (OSCE).

The best way to prepare for communication stations is to get together in a group of at least three, with one of you role-playing the part of a patient/relative, one playing the examiner, who can observe and assess, and one being the candidate. Five examples follow in this chapter, and you can see from their breadth that the scope for scenarios is huge. This should not daunt you; use these five scenarios as a tool to learn general communication principles, which you will then be able to apply to any situation. You can, of course, write your own scenarios for extra practice. By practising you will develop a stock of phrases that you feel comfortable using and you will improve your communication skills by learning from the feedback given to you by your 'examiner' and 'patient/relative'. Access to a video recorder during these sessions can be extremely useful, allowing you to watch and evaluate your own performance and think of ways in which to improve.

The specific skills for each type of communication station exemplified are described with that station. However, there are some general skills that need to be demonstrated in all communication stations. Non-verbal communication forms a large component of any interaction. You should sit directly facing the person you are talking to, leaning slightly forward, indicating your interest in the conversation. You should maintain eye contact with your 'patient/relative' and encourage him or her with non-verbal signs, for example a slight nod of the head. In the jargon this is known as active listening. Make sure that while the 'patient/relative' is talking you are listening and not simply thinking of the next thing to say; it will help you to use other skills such as summarizing and reflecting back if you actually heard what was said! Try to become comfortable with silence, using it as an effective communication tool, for example by giving your 'patient/relative' time to accommodate to some bad news. Modify the tone of your voice to match your communication aim, and at all costs avoid confrontation.

Should your 'patient/relative' become aggressive or confrontational, allow him or her to vent his/her anger and complete what he/she wants to say. Once he/she has finished, convey that you understand how he/she is feeling or that you are sorry that he/she is feeling that way and then go on to negotiate. Be confident, clear and polite to whoever you are communicating with.

Remember at the end of all communication stations to summarize to your 'patient/relative' what has been discussed or agreed upon to help draw the communication to a close. Always check that the person you have communicated with is satisfied with your discussion and does not wish to raise any further points or ask further questions.

In the same way that a summary draws a conversation to a close, 'sign-posting' draws an aspect of a conversation to a close and is also a very useful tool. It ensures that the examiner knows you are about to carry out a particular step on the mark-sheet and facilitates transition to the next aspect of conversation.

The role-player's global rating will be a measure of how satisfied he or she felt in the role with your conversation. The role-player will be assessing whether you met his/her needs, and whether you would make the kind of doctor/colleague he/she would feel comfortable talking to about a difficult issue. Establishing rapport with your role-player is crucial to scoring high global marks. The examiner's global rating, in contrast, is more a reflection of your demonstration of different communication skills and your factual accuracy.

With practice, communication stations can become relatively easy, if not predictable. Even if you find yourself somewhat ignorant about the topic you are faced with, you can pick up a lot of points by focusing on the communication aspects. It is perfectly acceptable to tell the role-player that you are unable to give him or her the information he/she requires at that time, but that you will endeavour to find out and you will let him/her know. Practise with your peers in small groups, attend communication sessions and, if you are feeling very keen, there are some interesting about communication books that you can read.

Remember, it's good to talk!

ENGLISH AS A SECOND LANGUAGE

You are a pre-registration house officer (PRHO) in general practice. Michael Rodriguez, a Spanish-speaking student, has come to see you. He speaks just a little English, and you do not speak Spanish. Please explore his presenting complaint and form an appropriate management plan with your patient.

Conduct of the interview

Delivers effective introduction and establishes rapport
Confirms patient's name and age
Establishes level to which patient speaks English
Explores presenting complaint and patient's concerns
Offers appropriate medical advice to relieve symptoms
Offers follow-up

General use of the following communication skills

Rephrases questions/statements to aid patient's understanding
Uses non-verbal/visual means of aiding communication, for example by drawing or pointing at objects
Avoids being patronizing
Maintains rapport with the patient
Summarises and checks understanding

Global marks

Examiner global rating
Role-player global rating

KEY TIPS 🗝

Communicating with patients who speak little or no English is something that most doctors will experience in their careers, and it is important to have the necessary skills, as any misunderstanding could be potentially detrimental to your patient's care.

In the above scenario Michael speaks a little English and has presented to you with coryzal symptoms suggestive of a common cold. Michael's concerns are that he needs antibiotics and your advice to him should be that he rests and takes paracetamol for a few days, returning with someone who can act as an interpreter if these measures fail. You must ensure that your 'patient' understands what dose of paracetamol he should take and how often; you can use diagrams, for example of a clock to indicate dose times, to help you. You should also write down the details of drug treatment, other measures and follow-up arrangements, as Michael may be able to show these to someone who can act as an interpreter. Overall, be cautious with medication, as you may have an incorrect understanding of the presenting complaint and cannot be sure that the 'patient' does not have any allergies.

Always offer the 'patient' follow-up, as a safety net. Using simple words, short sentences, varying your vocabulary and using non-verbal communication will be helpful in this station. Just be creative! But, using pigeon English yourself or simply speaking slower and louder will probably be considered patronizing and add little to your score.

DELIVERING DIFFICULT NEWS

You are a PRHO in an outpatient clinic, seeing Mrs Jones, a 35-year-old lady who has seen your colleague previously with joint pains and stiffness in the hands. The results of blood tests and X-rays suggest a diagnosis of rheumatoid arthritis. Please deliver this news to Mrs Jones.

Conduct of the interview

Delivers effective introduction and establishes rapport
Confirms patient's name and age
Confirms patient's expectations of the interview and understanding of the situation so far (is she expecting bad news?)
Gives an effective warning shot
Delivers news
Elicits patient's concerns and worries
Agrees on a plan
Summarizes, checking for understanding
Concludes consultation effectively

General use of the following communication skills

Uses open and closed questions
Avoids using medical jargon
Encourages patient to ask questions
Paces information – uses silence
Demonstrates empathy both verbally and non-verbally
Maintains rapport with the patient
Accuracy of medical information

Global marks

Examiner global rating
Role-player global rating

KEY TIPS

This station assesses your ability to deliver difficult news to a patient, a very important skill as a doctor. The severity of the news you will be delivering may vary from informing a relative of the death of a patient to giving a patient a diagnosis of chronic disease. Below are some useful phrases for success in this station; the scenario above will be used to exemplify. Of course you should only use sentences/phrases that you are comfortable with, and you will discover these through practising scenarios.

Hello Mrs Jones. I am Dr X. I believe you saw my colleague Dr Y last time you came. Could you remind me of your age? What do you do? Who's at home with you? *These questions are important to establish rapport, and also the information you learn may affect your conduct of the interview.*

How have things been? Could you just go over again what was troubling you? How did it all start?

What were you expecting to hear today?

We have the results back from your blood tests and X-rays. I'm sorry to say that the news is not good/is serious/is bad.

This must be very hard for you, I know it is a shock.

Do you know anything about rheumatoid arthritis? Would you like me to tell you a bit about it?

What are your main worries at this time? *(Mrs Jones may be a painter and mother of three, or may have a sister with debilitating rheumatoid arthritis.)*

There is treatment available which will ease the pain and stiffness, and slow down the progression of the disease. Many people do very well on these tablets. I would like you to start taking these tablets today and to see me again in 2 weeks.

If you need to contact me, you can phone me here. I'd be happy to speak to you on the telephone/see you again. You could come back with your partner. *It is important here to plan treatment, foster realistic hope, and also offer availability.*

I'll just summarize what we've talked about today. *This is sign-posting that you are about to summarize, so that the examiner can tick the box!*

I'm so sorry that I had to inform you of this news. Are you all right to get home? Is there anything further I can help you with now?

Do not be put off if the 'patient' does not seem too distressed; in reality, different people respond to the same news in very different ways. Your response and interview must reflect this.

Conversely, if the 'patient' is very distressed, do not be too reluctant to continue; your agenda is to demonstrate your ability to conduct an interview of this kind. If necessary, you could say something like, 'I know that you're upset, but there are a few things I need to ask you'. However, just be careful that you do not appear to be going through the mark-sheet in too mechanical a way, and that you are responding to your 'patient's' needs – striking a balance is the key, as it is for qualified doctors.

CROSS-CULTURAL COMMUNICATION

You are a PRHO in general practice. A Muslim woman who is a type 1 diabetic on insulin has just seen the nurse practitioner with a urinary tract infection, and the nurse has also noted a high blood glucose measurement. The patient needs antibiotics for the infection, and the nurse, suspecting the high blood sugars to be due to intercurrent illness, advises her to increase the insulin for a few days. However, she then explains to the nurse practitioner that because it is Ramadan, she has been omitting her morning insulin as she is fasting during daylight hours. You have been asked to explore the situation with the patient and give appropriate medical advice.

Conduct of the interview
Delivers effective introduction and establishes rapport
Confirms patient's name and age
Establishes reason for interview, and elicits patient's ideas and expectations
Establishes patient's religious/cultural group
Establishes implications of religious practice, i.e. that it is Ramadan, and confirms that she is observing Ramadan
Establishes patient's dietary and insulin routine during Ramadan
Elicits patient's beliefs and values with regard to observing Ramadan
Explores clinical situation with patient
Gives accurate medical advice
Negotiates an agreed outcome

General use of the following communication skills
Expresses positive attitude and respect towards patient's beliefs and values
Does not appear patronizing or judgemental
Summarizes appropriately
Checks for understanding
Maintains rapport with patient
Encourages patient to ask questions

Global marks
Examiner global rating
Role-player global rating

KEY TIPS ━●

This station assesses your ability to understand the implication of cultural issues on the health of your patients, and to negotiate a course of action that satisfies both your agenda as a doctor and the patient's religious/cultural needs. A basic knowledge of major religious and cultural practices is useful in this sort of communication, as it may allow you to find a solution that will be acceptable to both parties. For example, in the scenario opposite, you could mention to the 'patient' that exceptions on medical grounds are permitted whilst observing Ramadan, and suggest to her that she could discuss this further with a leader at her mosque. In general, encouraging the 'patient' to discuss the situation with someone from his/her cultural/religious group before coming back to talk to you proves to be a good solution.

The key skills to demonstrate in this station are open-mindedness, respect and a willingness to understand and accommodate. Of course, use of the general communication skills outlined in the introduction is required too. There are many possible scenarios for this station. Two examples are that you could be discussing a blood transfusion with a patient who is a Jehovah's Witness, or the need for post mortem and the resultant delay in burial of a Jewish patient who has just died.

EXPLANATION OF AN OPERATIVE PROCEDURE

You are the surgical PRHO on-call, and the ward sister has asked you to speak to Mrs Smith, who is an elective patient for a laparoscopic cholecystectomy. She is going to have the procedure under a general anaesthetic. She is quite anxious and wishes to discuss the events of the next day with you. Please discuss pre-operative and post-operative management with her, and the possible complications of surgery.

Conduct of the interview

Delivers effective introduction and establishes rapport
Confirms patient's name and age
States the purpose of the interview
Elicits patient's own understanding of the operative events
Elicits patient's main concerns
Explains the need to fast pre-operatively
Explains pre-operative medication (benzodiazepines/antibiotics)
Explains how the patient will be anaesthetized
Appropriate explanation of the surgical procedure, including possibility of conversion to open cholecystectomy
Explains recovery room procedure (oxygen, blood pressure monitoring etc.)
Discusses post-operative analgesia and anti-emetics
Explains common post-operative complications

General use of the following communication skills

Establishes and maintains rapport with the patient
Encourages patient to ask questions, and addresses patient's concerns
Avoids using medical jargon
Accuracy of medical information
Summarizes appropriately
Checks for understanding

Global marks

Examiner global rating
Role-player global rating

KEY TIPS 🔑

With situations like this, both in the OSCE and in reality, it is well worth asking the patient at the outset what his or her main concerns are and what he/she wishes to know. This will enable you to focus your discussion on the patient's needs, increasing his/her satisfaction and saving you time. If, for example, the patient's main concern is pain, you should focus your discussion on analgesia, only briefly covering other aspects as required. It is also worth clarifying what his/her current understanding is so that you pitch your discussion at an appropriate level. You may find, on the one hand, that your patient is unclear about what operation he or she is having or, on the other, that he/she wishes to discuss exactly which anaesthetic agent will be used. The role-players in the OSCE are there to help you, and if you give them the opportunity, they will help direct your discussion to enable you to gain the most marks. Your 'patient' may have been armed with a particular concern, for example having to see the operation whilst under epidural anaesthesia, and the mark scheme will include points for eliciting and addressing that concern. Be courteous and polite, establish rapport and ask the 'patient' during the conversation if there is anything else he/she wishes to know about or discuss. The main tip here is to follow the role-player's agenda not your own. In this scenario, Mrs Smith wishes to have an overall explanation of what will happen, as she has never had an operation before, and is also particularly concerned about being in pain and developing a deep vein thrombosis.

Although the exact mark-sheet for each type of operation may vary, the overall scheme will be as opposite. In your discussion of analgesia, include all the possible methods – epidural analgesia, patient-controlled analgesia, intravenous opiates, intramuscular/subcutaneous opiates, oral analgesia, suppositories, patches and, if appropriate, the side effects. Explain to the 'patient' that the anaesthetist and pain team together will manage his/her analgesia. If your role-player is to have an epidural, a discussion of side effects is particularly relevant, and you should inform him/her about the possibility of headache, numbness and autonomic blockade affecting blood pressure and bowel and bladder function. With some surgical procedures there are specific post-operative measures that are taken (for example having a urinary catheter with bladder irrigation post-transurethral resection of the prostate (TURP) and you should inform your role-player of these when you discuss post-operative management. There are, of course, procedure-specific complications (bile duct complications in gall bladder surgery, for example). However, if you discuss pain, bleeding and infection, and mention that a more senior doctor will explain the complications in detail when he or she comes to gain consent for surgery, you will get the marks. Although as a PRHO you cannot gain consent for surgery, gaining informed consent generally is a concept you should be familiar with and in some OSCEs you may be asked to demonstrate this in these sorts of stations.

The best way to learn about operative management is by spending some time on surgical ward rounds. Here you will encounter pre-operative patients who have been fasted and are being consented, and post-operative patients who are receiving analgesia and anti-emetics. Attending a surgical pre-assessment clinic will demonstrate to you the sorts of concerns people commonly have about operations and will prepare you for the questions your role-player might ask you in the OSCE. Your description of the actual surgical procedure is, of course, easier if you have seen it in theatre; however, only common operations are likely to be used as OSCE scenarios, namely laparoscopic cholecystectomy, hernia repair, varicose vein stripping, TURP, and hip and knee replacements.

EXPLANATION OF AN INVESTIGATIVE PROCEDURE

You are a surgical PRHO assisting in your consultant's outpatient clinic. Your consultant has just seen an elderly male patient who has presented with a 2-month history of rectal bleeding and weight loss. Your consultant has booked an urgent colonoscopy to help diagnose the cause. Your consultant has asked you to discuss the procedure with the patient, and to address any concerns he may have.

Conduct of the interview
Delivers effective introduction and establishes rapport
Confirms patient's name and age
States the purpose of the interview
Elicits patient's own understanding of colonoscopy
Elicits patient's main concerns
Correctly explains bowel preparation to the patient
Explains the possibility of intravenous sedation
Describes the procedure itself, including the need to take biopsies
Explains the post-procedure recovery period
Explains to the patient that he will need someone to accompany him home if he receives sedation
Explains the risks of the procedure
Addresses the patient's concern about receiving the result

General use of the following communication skills
Establishes and maintains rapport with the patient
Encourages patient to ask questions and addresses his concerns
Avoids using medical jargon
Accuracy of medical information
Summarizes appropriately
Checks for understanding

 ## Global marks

Examiner global rating
Role-player global rating

KEY TIPS ⚍●

Explaining an investigative procedure is essentially the same as explaining an operative procedure, and the principles outlined for the previous station apply to this station. Other common investigations which you should be able to explain are: general X-ray, oesophago-gastro-duodenoscopy (OGD), flexible sigmoidoscopy, computerized tomography (CT) scan, magnetic resonance imaging (MRI) scan, barium enema, barium swallow/ meal/ follow-through, ventilation/perfusion scan, ultrasound, lung function tests and echocardiogram. If you are not sure what is involved in any of these investigations, you could go along to the relevant departments and observe them. It need not take long and will give you a clear understanding both for your explanation in an OSCE and also for your practice as a PRHO.

Although the exact mark-sheet for each type of investigation may vary, the overall scheme will be as outlined opposite. Essentially, you need to introduce yourself, state the purpose of the discussion and establish exactly what the role-player wishes to know and what his/her main concerns are. You then explain any preparation the procedure may require, for example bowel clear-outs or having a full bladder for a pelvic ultrasound. The next step of the explanation is about the procedure itself, how it takes place and what is involved, and finally you explain the post-procedure implications (e.g. passing barium rectally after a barium enema, or transport home after intravenous sedation) and any complications. Learn the common risks and complications for each type of procedure and, if you want to sound really slick, memorize a couple of statistics – for example the risk of perforation during an OGD is less than 1/1000.

In this particular scenario, your role-player is concerned about the pain of the procedure, possible indignity and how he will be informed of the result. You should reassure him that, although uncomfortable, it is not actually painful and that there is the possibility of intravenous sedation. You should also reassure your role-player that the endoscopist is used to performing colonoscopies, and although it is natural for him to feel embarrassed, the endoscopist will not be. Finally, explain to him that he will be seen back in clinic very shortly after the procedure to have the results explained and, if necessary, further investigations or treatment planned. Be sensitive to the fact that your role-player probably has some idea that a neoplastic process is a possible diagnosis.

SECTION 8: PERSONAL AND PROFESSIONAL DEVELOPMENT

SECTION 8: PERSONAL AND PROFESSIONAL DEVELOPMENT

The increased scrutiny of the medical profession over recent years has meant that medical schools have to be absolutely sure that graduates have real and measurable competency in *all* the skills they will need as junior doctors. Some skills are easy to categorize, for example physical examination, and it should be obvious from the instructions that you are given for these in the objective structured clinical examination (OSCE) stations which category is being tested. Being a competent junior doctor is, however, a complex business requiring many skills and talents that cannot be easily defined and categorized, falling broadly into the rather vague domain of personal and professional development. As undergraduate curricula and assessment are modernized, testing personal and professional development is becoming a significant component of assessment at finals, and it cannot be ignored.

Stations testing personal and professional development will often involve complex clinical, ethical, interpersonal and legal scenarios. Such stations require you to demonstrate your attitudes, team-working skills, use of legal and ethical principles in decision making, communication and empathy; and assess how these are integrated to manage emotional and demanding situations. Evidence suggests that people find it harder to behave in a professionally correct manner the more complex and demanding the situation is; therefore the scenarios in the OSCE may simulate very difficult situations, to see whether your attitudes are appropriate, even under pressure. Some of the attitudes being tested include:

- being respectful and non-judgemental with all patients,
- respecting the rights of patients to be involved in decision making about their own care,
- showing respect towards colleagues and their views,
- demonstrating an insight into your own limitations and the capacity to learn from other professionals.

Some types of stations will test your ability to practise evidence-based health care, clinical governance and health promotion, all of which are very important in today's National Health Service (NHS) and required for best patient care. Other types of stations will assess your administrative skills and ability to function within the NHS setting, for example communicating over the telephone or in written form, requesting or organizing investigations, completing prescription charts, interpreting investigation results, demonstrating skills in information technology etc.

In this chapter we have included a selection of personal and professional development stations. The scenarios included are discussing resuscitation status, advanced directives, assessing speech, evidence-based health care, health promotion, and communicating with a colleague. Essentially, scenarios can be based on anything that you may encounter or be required to do as a junior doctor. Therefore, further examples are making a verbal/written referral to another team/doctor, discussing concerns about a colleague's competence/behaviour with a senior colleague, talking to a patient who wishes to self-discharge from hospital, and discussing your disagreement about a senior colleague's management of a patient with him or her.

In a sense, therefore, specific learning for these stations is difficult, and perhaps the most useful preparation is to spend some time shadowing junior doctors, gaining an insight into the range of situations they encounter, and what personal attributes and professional skills are needed. Good sources of reference would also be *Tomorrow's Doctors* and *Good Medical Practice*, both of which are guiding the new curricula and available on the General Medical Council (GMC) website (www.gmc-uk.org). As always, write a range of scenarios for practice, guided by your medical school course objectives and past/sample OSCE stations, and keep practising them!

Reflecting on the ideal/required attitudes, and on your own attitudes and skills, is useful. For example, you could ask yourself the following questions: How do I show respect for other members of the team? What things that I say and do reflect my non-judgemental attitudes? What things that I say and do make me seem judgemental? Once you have reflected on these ideas personally, extend your reflection by discussion with your colleagues. Pick up ideas from them, using their feedback and thoughts to enhance your own professional attitudes and skills. Practise scenarios in groups, and discuss whether the personal attributes and professional skills expected of junior doctors were demonstrated; if they were not, discuss what the 'doctor' could have done differently and how. You may find that you need to re-work the scenario several times, each time incorporating the ideas of the group, in order to achieve a model for a successful performance. You may also find it useful to seek guidance from practising doctors, other health care professionals (for example palliative care nurses) and communication teachers.

We have made the mark-sheets in this chapter fairly detailed and have listed the general/communication skills that you should demonstrate, as well as the individual steps that you need to go through in each scenario. In a sense, therefore, global marks in these stations are for demonstrating the general/communication skills and behaviours that are listed.

DO NOT RESUSCITATE ORDER

You are the medical senior house officer (SHO) on-call. Mr Smith, aged 78, has advanced metastatic cancer of the bladder. He was admitted with a chest infection, has been on the ward for 2 days, and has been too poorly to communicate clearly until now. The team has indicated in the medical notes that his prognosis is weeks rather than months, and that in view of his significant co-existing ischaemic heart disease, cardiopulmonary resuscitation is inappropriate. However, they have not been able to discuss this with him, and a 'do not resuscitate order' has not been signed. Today his symptoms are well controlled and he appears alert. The nurse in charge has asked you to discuss his resuscitation status with him.

Conduct of the interview

Delivers appropriate introduction, and establishes rapport
Assesses patient's 'competence' to make decisions
Checks patient's understanding of his situation/prognosis
Gives an effective warning shot
Explains the need for a resuscitation decision
Acknowledges the distress the discussion may cause
Elicits patient's beliefs and values with regard to resuscitation
Gives clear and honest appraisal of prognosis
Gives clear and honest appraisal of probable resuscitation outcome
Asks the patient whether or not he wishes to be for cardiopulmonary resuscitation
Negotiates an agreed outcome
Checks understanding of patient's decision with a clear but sensitive summary
Offers opportunity to discuss with relatives
Offers opportunity to talk further

General use of the following communication skills

Encourages the patient to ask questions and addresses his concerns
Paces information – uses silence
Avoids using medical jargon, and gives accurate information
Demonstrates empathy both verbally and non-verbally
Is sensitive to patient's responses and reacts appropriately
Expresses positive attitude and respect towards patient's beliefs and values
Maintains rapport with the patient

 ## Global marks

Examiner global rating
Role-player global rating

KEY TIPS •━●

This is a difficult scenario to simulate during your OSCE preparation, but it is useful to get some practice at these sorts of stations before the OSCE. There is a balance to strike between your agenda for the interview and being sensitive to the 'patient's' needs and reactions – a skill that will only develop with practice.

Patients cannot make decisions about their care unless they are deemed 'competent' to do so at the time of decision making; this applies to end-of-life decision making as much as it does to giving consent for procedures. Therefore the first thing to do in your interview is to assess whether the 'patient' is indeed 'competent' to make the decision about resuscitation status, a decision that needs to be 'informed'. You need to make sure that the 'patient' is able to understand and retain any information you have given about his/her health status and prognosis. He/she also needs to be able to use and consider this information in his/her decision-making process, weighing up the risks and benefits.

In many ways, some of the communication skills required in this sort of station are similar to the delivering difficult news station in the previous chapter (pp. 130–31); it is worth looking again at that mark-sheet and key tips section. For example, in both stations you should assess the 'patient's' understanding of his/her situation early on in the discussion, and give a warning shot prior to introducing the difficult topic. An effective warning shot in this station might be 'I have something very important and serious to discuss with you'.

It is vital that you check that you have understood the 'patient's' decision and wishes exactly. This has to be done with some sensitivity, and is best done by summarizing the discussion. Deciding on resuscitation status is very frightening for some patients, and they may wish to talk to their partner/family about it before making a final decision. You should always offer this opportunity, as well as offering to talk to them about it again even if they have formed a final decision. This will make it feel less final and frightening, and helps you conclude the discussion, but it is not an offer to go back on the decision and therefore needs to be handled carefully. A suggestion might be: 'Thank you Mr Smith. I know this has been a difficult discussion for you. I can come and see how you are later, once you have had a chance to let it sink in'.

Other scenarios that assess skills similar to this one include: discussing whether to stop feeding a grown-up child in a persistent vegetative state with his/her parents, or turning off a ventilator in an intensive care setting. In these cases, however, the patient is 'non-competent' and therefore the best interests of the patient as judged by the medical team, informed by the input of family, will drive the decision.

TALKING TO RELATIVES ABOUT ADVANCED DIRECTIVES

You are a medical SHO and have admitted Mr Jones with a severe chest infection. He is 44 years old, has motor neurone disease, and is unable to talk or move. He has a written advanced directive that he should not be resuscitated in the event of a cardiac arrest, and that you should not take any measure that would prolong his life. His wife, whom you have not met before, has asked to see you. She is very distressed; she thinks he has made a mistake with regard to the advanced directive and is demanding he is kept alive as long as possible.

Conduct of the interview

Delivers appropriate introduction, and establishes rapport
Confirms Mrs Jones' identity and relationship to Mr Jones
Listens to Mrs Jones' ideas and concerns
Checks Mrs Jones' understanding of the advanced directive
Acknowledges that relatives' wishes are important
Explains the need for doctors to act according to the patient's best interests when a patient is 'non-competent'
Explains in a clear but sensitive manner that fulfilling an advanced directive is a legal requirement for doctors, and this may mean that relatives' wishes are not met
Acknowledges that fulfilling the advanced directive may cause distress to Mrs Jones
Offers her an opportunity to talk to a more senior member of the medical team
Does not raise her hopes that the decision can be changed
Checks Mrs Jones has understood the decision by summarizing in a clear but sensitive manner
Ends discussion appropriately

General use of the following communication skills

Encourages Mrs Jones to ask questions, and addresses her concerns
Gives correct and accurate information
Paces information – uses silence
Demonstrates empathy both verbally and non-verbally
Expresses positive attitude and respect towards Mrs Jones' feelings
Maintains rapport with Mrs Jones

 ## Global marks

Examiner global rating
Role-player global rating

KEY TIPS ⚬━●

Talking to relatives is a common scenario in OSCEs. However, this is a particularly difficult situation, requiring you to have legal knowledge about advanced directives and also to communicate sensitively in an emotionally demanding situation. You can expect relatives sometimes to express anger towards you as a member of the medical team, and it will be useful preparation to think in advance of phrases you would use to try to diffuse anger and to soothe a distressed relative without raising false hope. Examples might be: 'I do understand that this is very difficult for you ... ' (pause) ' ... it is ok to be angry. This is a very difficult time for you, and together we must do what is best for your husband. We will always be happy to talk to you about any concerns that you have'. As always, make sure you practise and use phrases that you are comfortable with. A useful tip is to remember to be personal in your discussion; do not say 'doctors have to' or 'in the interests of the patient' – it shows a general lack of compassion and makes the relatives feel that their loved ones mean nothing special to you.

The ethical and legal principles used in decision making in this scenario are confidentiality, the 'non-competent' patient, and advanced directives. These are common areas to test, and it is worth knowing the necessary legal facts and the GMC guidance. The legal right to medical confidentiality is a prima facie one. However, there are some situations in which confidentiality may or must be overridden, and doctors need to be aware of these. As a general rule, give any information to the patient first and ensure you have his/her consent to talk to relatives before giving them information (the exception being if the patient is 'non-competent', as in this case). Always confirm the identity of the relative you are talking to in a sensitive manner, for example 'As you know, before I can divulge any information, I need to be sure who I am speaking to. Forgive me, but can I ask you to tell me who you are and what your relationship is to Mr Jones?'

In some scenarios you may be faced with role-players asking for information that you are unable to give, either because the patient is 'competent' and you have not yet had the opportunity to ask his/her permission to talk to a third party, or because you have been expressly forbidden by the patient to talk to anyone else.

Relatives and loved ones (partner, friend, carer, support worker or advocate) often seek to influence the decisions of doctors. It is only right that their ideas are heard and, where possible, incorporated into the care of their loved ones, unless you have reason to believe that the patient would not have wanted those individuals to be involved. They, after all, know the patient best and can give very useful information about his/her values and wishes. However, the final responsibility for determining whether a procedure or decision is in a 'non-competent' patient's best interests lies with the medical team. Best interests are not just best medical interests, but include factors such as the patient's wishes and beliefs when competent, his/her current wishes, general well-being, dignity and spiritual and religious welfare.

The use of advanced directives acts as a guide to ensure that the doctor is doing what the patient wished for, and doctors are legally compelled to follow advanced directives whether written or verbal.

Global marks in this station, as for the last, are for your ability to demonstrate empathy whilst tackling an emotionally challenging situation. Mrs Jones has to be made aware of how any decisions about her husband's care will be made, but this should be conveyed to her in a way that does not result in a breakdown in the relationship between her and the team. The examiner will also be looking for a minimum basic knowledge of the legal and ethical issues involved.

Other scenarios to practise include talking to the parents of a young man with a non-recoverable head injury, where brain death has been established and your team has decided to withdraw life support; or talking to the relatives of a patient with advanced Alzheimer's dementia about a 'do not resuscitate' decision.

HEALTH PROMOTION

You are a SHO seeing a patient in a diabetes follow-up clinic. Ms Brown is 68 years old and was diagnosed with diabetes during a hospital admission following a fall 6 weeks ago. She was commenced on oral hypoglycaemic treatment. Her general practitioner has written to you voicing his concern that she is only taking her treatment when her blood sugar gets too high (>20 mmol/L). She has also been going to a specialist in natural medicine, who is treating her diabetes with herbal remedies. Please discuss her diabetes care with her.

Conduct of the interview

Makes appropriate introduction, and establishes rapport
Explains the purpose of the interview
Checks the patient's understanding of diabetes
Checks the patient's understanding of the importance of maintaining good glycaemic control
Elicits the patient's concerns and worries about the disease
Elicits the patient's concerns and worries about the treatment
Elicits the patient's beliefs and values with regard to mainstream medicine
Explores how Ms Brown has been taking her medication
Gives a clear explanation of diabetes and why it is important to maintain good glycaemic control
Discusses lifestyle changes that can help glycaemic control
Suggests alternative methods of support or help (e.g. community diabetic nurse, Diabetes UK)
Negotiates a joint treatment plan which accommodates the patient's ideas
Makes an appropriate plan for follow-up
Summarizes appropriately

General use of the following communication skills

Is accurate in information given
Avoids using medical jargon
Encourages the patient to ask questions
Checks for understanding
Does not appear patronizing or judgemental
Is respectful towards the patient's beliefs and values
Maintains rapport with the patient

 ## Global marks

Examiner global rating
Role-player global rating

KEY TIPS ⚊●

All doctors have a responsibility to prevent disease and to promote the health and well-being of their patients, actively seeking opportunities to practise health promotion even if the health issues are unrelated to their current problems. This station is not just testing whether you can effectively deliver health promotion, but is also assessing your consultation skills. As doctors, we usually have our own agenda for a consultation, and in this scenario the doctor's agenda would be to inform Ms Brown that she must take her oral hypoglycaemic agents as prescribed, and possibly to stop taking the herbal remedies. However, if you use this doctor-centred approach, the likelihood is that Ms Brown will not change her health behaviour. To achieve 'concordance', you must use a patient-centred approach in your consultation. You need to explore Ms Brown's own understanding of diabetes and of her treatment, and what her own feelings are towards it. It may be that she has some misconceptions which you can help resolve, or it may be that she has some quite firmly held health beliefs about conventional medicine and prefers an alternative approach. Her views need to be incorporated and you need to make a joint plan which achieves a compromise, and which she will be happy with – a treatment plan that she is likely to adhere to. It may be that this joint plan is sub-optimal or not ideal for the management of diabetes, but if you do not achieve a compromise that the 'patient' is happy with, you will probably not gain her concordance with any treatment at all. Always offer the 'patient' a follow-up meeting; this not only acts as a safety net, but also shows that you realize that health promotion is not a one-off activity.

Health promotion stations are likely to be based on key public health issues such as smoking, excess alcohol intake, exercise, hypertension, obesity, high cholesterol, childhood immunizations and diabetes. It is worth writing mark-sheets for these scenarios for further practice. Knowing what resources are available in the hospital and in the community, within both the NHS and the voluntary sector, is useful for all health promotion stations – you could make a list of resources for the key health promotion targets.

ASSESSING SPEECH DIFFICULTIES

Mrs Williams is 68 years old and has some difficulties with her speech. Please assess her speech problem and suggest a diagnosis.

Conduct of the interview

Makes appropriate introduction of self
Gains consent for the interview
Explains the purpose of the interview
Attempts to establish the patient's name
Attempts to test the patient's orientation in time and place
Gives opportunity for the patient to identify her own speech difficulty
Checks for dysarthria (e.g. asks the patient to say 'baby hippopotamus')
Checks for expressive dysphasia
Checks for receptive dysphasia
Checks for nominal dysphasia (shows the patient common objects and asks her to name them, e.g. pen or watch)
Checks for dysgraphia (asks the patient to write a sentence)

General use of the following communication skills

Moves at a pace that is comfortable for the patient, i.e. does not rush or interrupt her
If appropriate, rephrases questions/statements to aid the patient's understanding
Demonstrates understanding and empathy towards the patient's difficulties
Acknowledges the patient's distress or discomfort

Global marks

Examiner global rating
Role-player global rating

KEY TIPS

This station not only tests whether you can distinguish between the different types of speech difficulty (namely dysarthria, receptive dysphasia and expressive dysphasia), but also tests your professional attitudes towards disability. Speech difficulties are usually secondary to a cerebrovascular accident (CVA). They can also be part of other disease processes such as dementia, depression and parkinsonism, but you are much less likely to be asked about these.

It is worth remembering that there is not a whole ream of complicated neurological tests to perform in this station; the global marks are for your sensitivity, patience, understanding and empathy towards the patient's difficulty. Therefore it will lose you marks simply to run through a physical neurological examination, neglecting to demonstrate the above attitudes. The key to making a diagnosis in this station is just listening; hard to do if you are rushing through lots of questions or tests, or busy thinking about what you are going to say or do next!

Start with a clear introduction and description of what you are doing. For example you could use a phrase like 'Hello. My name is Jane Brown and, if it is okay, I am going to check out the difficulty you seem to be having with your speech. Is that okay? Now, first, can you tell me your name and whatever you can about the problem you are having?' Next, ask the patient to name some objects for you and try to ascertain what you think the difficulty is: is he/she having difficulty understanding you (receptive dysphasia), difficulty articulating the words (dysarthria), difficulty finding the right words (expressive dysphasia), or difficulty getting the right words on prompting (nominal dysphasia)? Whilst the patient is writing a sentence, you should observe for which is the dominant hand, the side of any weakness, and other obvious neurological signs, for example an intention tremor or pill-rolling.

If you are unsure about what you have heard, ask the patient to repeat him or herself or to perform the task again. This has to be done sensitively; patients with good cognitive function and poor speech can be terribly distressed and frustrated, and patients with CVAs and dementia, for example, can be emotionally labile. Acknowledging distress can be simply done by saying 'I realize this must be terribly distressing for you. Would you like me to stop for a while?'

The diagnosis in speech difficulty is likely to be a CVA, and you would be expected to know in which region the lesion is. The dominant hemisphere for speech in right-handed people and in 50 per cent of left-handed people is the left hemisphere. Check for other clues, such as the side of any paralysis. Pure expressive dysphasia tends to result from lesions in the frontal lobe (Broca's area), and receptive dysphasia from lesions in the temporo-parietal lobes (Wernicke's area).

EVIDENCE-BASED HEALTH CARE

Structured viva format station

In this station, we consider research by The Diabetes Control and Complications Trial Research Group, a trial looking into whether intensively treating insulin-dependent diabetes mellitus has any impact on its long-term complications. Please read the summary methods and results sections of the paper. You will then be asked some questions by the examiners.

DCCT Research Group. The effect of intensive treatment of diabetes on the development and progression of long-term complications in insulin-dependent diabetes mellitus. *New Engl J Med* 1993; **329**:977–86.

1. Why do you think the authors chose to study this area?
2. This is a randomized control trial; where does this sort of evidence sit in the hierarchy of published papers?
3. Considering the methods section:
   Was the assignment of patients to treatment groups randomized?
   Were all patients who entered the trial properly accounted for at its conclusion?
   To what extent was blinding carried out (patients, doctors, study personnel)?
   Aside from the experimental intervention, were the groups treated equally?
4. Considering the results section:
   What is the ratio of rates (treatment group:control group) and therefore the relative risk?
   How large was the treatment effect in terms of relative risk?
   How precise was the treatment effect (i.e. how wide was the confidence interval)?
5. Are these clinically important outcomes?
6. How would you explain this evidence to a diabetic patient with poor glycaemic control?

 ## Global marks

Examiner global rating

KEY TIPS ━●

This station tests your ability to understand and interpret research published in medical journals, and to critically evaluate and appropriately apply it to the care of patients either at an individual or population-wide level; it tests your ability to practise evidence-based health care. These sorts of stations are likely to be a structured viva format, which means that you will have some time to evaluate and consider a paper, either in its full or summary form, before being asked questions on it by one or two examiners. Evidenced-based health care stations can be combined with testing one of the other professional competencies, and so you may expect these stations to be based on papers considering health promotion areas, for example smoking, or areas where there may be ethical dilemmas, such as prenatal screening.

The questions used in this viva are based on those listed in:

Sackett DL. *Evidence-based Medicine: How to Practise and Teach EBM*, 2nd edn. London: Churchill Livingstone, 2000.

If your final OSCE includes stations on evidence-based health care, it is well worth having a look at this book.

To be prepared for these stations, you should be able to:

- define basic statistical principles such as sensitivity, specificity, and the positive and negative predictive values of a diagnostic test;
- define the term prevalence, and explain the relationship between positive predictive value and prevalence when commenting on the value of a test;
- understand the terms absolute reduction in risk, number needed to treat, relative risk, odds ratio, null hypothesis, statistically significant, p-value, and the confidence interval in relation to intervention trials;
- define the terms random allocation, control group, completeness of follow-up, intention-to-treat analysis, blinding, and blinding with respect to a randomized controlled trial;
- explain how reliable evidence is effectively searched for and name some sources of information;
- describe the hierarchy of evidence for assessing the benefits of medical interventions.

If you feel you are unfamiliar with statistics and interpreting research, it is worth asking one of your statistics tutors to run a brief revision session with you and to bring along some papers for you to work on. You could also attend some hospital journal clubs, or look at some papers in small groups, for example the Scandinavian Simvastatin Survival Study about cholesterol. You may find that one of your colleagues is used to reading and interpreting academic papers and is good at these evidence-based health care stations; the benefit of working in groups is that you can learn from each other's strengths and weaknesses.

COMMUNICATING WITH A COLLEAGUE

You are a surgical pre-registration house officer (PRHO). A patient reports to you that a nurse has been ignoring her requests for an enema but has managed to attend to all the other patients in the bay. She feels that she is being discriminated against in some way and wishes to make a formal complaint. You have always found the nurse in question to be highly responsive and competent. You decide to discuss the incident with her, both in order to respond to the patient and in the hope of being able to resolve the issues informally.

Conduct of the interview

Makes appropriate introductory conversation
States the purpose of the interview
States the patient's complaint factually
Elicits colleague's response and perception of the incident
Negotiates and agrees a course of action with the colleague

General use of the following communication skills

Demonstrates active listening
Demonstrates empathy and respect, both verbally and non-verbally
Offers advice/support to the colleague
Avoids being judgemental, blaming or criticizing the colleague
Avoids colluding with the colleague or criticizing the patient
Maintains rapport with the colleague

Global marks

Examiner global rating
Role-player global rating

KEY TIPS

Developing effective interpersonal/communication skills with colleagues is crucial to surviving a medical career, during which many difficult situations and points of conflict are inevitable. The reality is that some people feel more at ease than others at tackling situations like this and, if open supportive negotiation is not quite your style, it is well worth learning, both for the OSCE and for your sanity as a PRHO!

This scenario tests your ability to address the patient's complaint without being accusatory to your 'colleague', who you respect. You may find that your 'colleague' is initially quite angry and feels that you are confronting him/her, and this is something you will need to address at the outset. Creating a supportive environment for the discussion will help in this regard and, if necessary, offer him/her your support and understanding, and explain your obligation to explore the patient's complaint and your desire to resolve the situation informally. Your 'colleague' may explain his/her difficulties with that particular patient to you. Using phrases such as 'I can see your point of view' or 'I hear what you are saying' is useful in acknowledging your 'colleague's' perspective; only after you have done this will you be able to offer any advice and agree a course of action. If appropriate, you could offer to help resolve the issue, for example by being present whilst he/she talks to the patient or ward sister. At no stage should you criticize the patient and collude with your 'colleague' (tempting though it may be), as your professional responsibility is to protect those under your care.

There are many possible variants to this scenario. You could, for example, be asked to negotiate the discharge of an elderly patient with the ward physiotherapist who feels that the patient's mobility is not yet good enough. Or, instead of a situation of confrontation, you may be required to encourage and support a colleague to perform a task that he or she feels unable to do.

GLOSSARY

ABPI:	ankle–brachial pressure index
A&E:	accident and emergency
ALS:	advanced life support
ASIS:	anterior superior iliac spine
A-V:	arterio-venous
β–hCG:	beta-human chorionic gonadotrophin
BLS:	basic life support
bpm:	beats per minute
BNF:	*British National Formulary*
CCF:	congestive cardiac failure
CD:	compact disc
COPD:	chronic obstructive pulmonary disease
CRP:	C-reactive protein
CT:	computerized tomography
CVA:	cerebrovascular accident
DIP:	distal interphalangeal
DKA:	diabetic ketoacidosis
ECG:	electrocardiogram
ENT:	ear, nose and throat
ESR:	erythrocyte sedimentation rate
FBC:	full blood count
GMC:	General Medical Council
GP:	general practitioner
GTN:	glyceryl trinitrate
i.v.:	intravenous
JVP:	jugular venous pressure
LFTs:	liver function tests
LMN:	lower motor neurone
MCP:	metacarpophalangeal
MI:	myocardial infarction
MRI:	magnetic resonance imaging
NG:	nasogastric
NHS:	National Health Service
OGD:	oesophago-gastro-duodenoscopy
OSCE:	objective structured clinical examination
PLAB:	Professional and Linguistics Assessment Board
PRHO:	pre-registration house officer
RA:	rheumatoid arthritis
SHO:	senior house officer
stat.:	immediately (shortened from the Latin *statim*)
TURP:	transurethral resection of prostate
UMN:	upper motor neurone

INDEX